FOREWORD

The collection of "Everything Will Be Okay" travel phrasebooks published by T&P Books is designed for people traveling abroad for tourism and business. The phrasebooks contain what matters most - the essentials for basic communication. This is an indispensable set of phrases to "survive" while abroad.

This phrasebook will help you in most cases where you need to ask something, get directions, find out how much something costs, etc. It can also resolve difficult communication situations where gestures just won't help.

This book contains a lot of phrases that have been grouped according to the most relevant topics. You'll also find a mini dictionary with useful words - numbers, time, calendar, colors...

Take "Everything Will Be Okay" phrasebook with you on the road and you'll have an irreplaceable traveling companion who will help you find your way out of any situation and teach you to not fear speaking with foreigners.

TABLE OF CONTENTS

T&P Books Publishing

T&P Books Publishing

PHRASEBOOK

— GERMAN —

THE MOST IMPORTANT PHRASES

This phrasebook contains
the most important
phrases and questions
for basic communication
Everything you need
to survive overseas

By Andrey Taranov

T&P BOOKS

Phrasebook + 250-word dictionary

English-German phrasebook & mini dictionary

By Andrey Taranov

The collection of "Everything Will Be Okay" travel phrasebooks published by T&P Books is designed for people traveling abroad for tourism and business. The phrasebooks contain what matters most - the essentials for basic communication. This is an indispensable set of phrases to "survive" while abroad.

You'll also find a mini dictionary with 250 useful words required for everyday communication - the names of months and days of the week, measurements, family members, and more.

T&P Books Publishing
www.tpbooks.com

ISBN: 978-1-78492-404-1

This book is also available in E-book formats.
Please visit www.tpbooks.com or the major online bookstores.

PRONUNCIATION

T&P phonetic alphabet	German example	English example

Vowels

T&P phonetic alphabet	German example	English example
[a]	Blatt	shorter than in ask
[ɐ]	Meister	nut
[e]	Melodie	elm, medal
[ɛ]	Herbst	man, bad
[ə]	Leuchte	driver, teacher
[ɔ]	Knopf	bottle, doctor
[o]	Operette	pod, John
[œ]	Förster	German Hölle
[ø]	nötig	eternal, church
[æ]	Los Angeles	candle, lamp
[i]	Spiel	shorter than in feet
[ɪ]	Absicht	big, America
[ʊ]	Skulptur	good, booklet
[u]	Student	book
[y]	Pyramide	fuel, tuna
[ʏ]	Eukalyptus	fuel, tuna

Consonants

T&P phonetic alphabet	German example	English example
[b]	Bibel	baby, book
[d]	Dorf	day, doctor
[f]	Elefant	face, food
[ʒ]	Ingenieur	forge, pleasure
[dʒ]	Jeans	joke, general
[j]	Interview	yes, New York
[g]	August	game, gold
[h]	Haare	home, have
[ç]	glücklich	humor
[x]	Kochtopf	as in Scots 'loch'
[k]	Kaiser	clock, kiss
[l]	Verlag	lace, people

T&P phonetic alphabet	German example	English example
[m]	Messer	magic, milk
[n]	Norden	name, normal
[ŋ]	Onkel	English, ring
[p]	Gespräch	pencil, private
[r]	Force majeure	rice, radio
[ʁ]	Kirche	French (guttural) R
[R]	fragen	uvular vibrant [r]
[s]	Fenster	city, boss
[t]	Foto	tourist, trip
[ts]	Gesetz	cats, tsetse fly
[ʃ]	Anschlag	machine, shark
[ʧ]	Deutsche	church, French
[w]	Sweater	vase, winter
[v]	Antwort	very, river
[z]	langsam	zebra, please

Diphthongs

[aɪ]	Speicher	tie, driver
[ɪa]	Miniatur	Kenya, piano
[ɪo]	Radio	New York
[jo]	Illustration	New York
[ɔɪ]	feucht	oil, boy, point
[ɪe]	Karriere	yesterday, yen

Other symbols used in transcription

[']	['a:bə]	primary stress
[ˌ]	['dɛŋkˌma:l]	secondary stress
[ʔ]	[oˈli:vənˌʔø:l]	glottal stop
[:]	['my:lə]	long-vowel mark
[·]	['ʀaɪzə·byˌʀo:]	interpunct

LIST OF ABBREVIATIONS

English abbreviations

ab.	-	about
adj	-	adjective
adv	-	adverb
anim.	-	animate
as adj	-	attributive noun used as adjective
e.g.	-	for example
etc.	-	et cetera
fam.	-	familiar
fem.	-	feminine
form.	-	formal
inanim.	-	inanimate
masc.	-	masculine
math	-	mathematics
mil.	-	military
n	-	noun
pl	-	plural
pron.	-	pronoun
sb	-	somebody
sing.	-	singular
sth	-	something
v aux	-	auxiliary verb
vi	-	intransitive verb
vi, vt	-	intransitive, transitive verb
vt	-	transitive verb

German abbreviations

f	-	feminine noun
f pl	-	feminine plural
f, n	-	feminine, neuter
m	-	masculine noun
m pl	-	masculine plural
m, f	-	masculine, feminine
m, n	-	masculine, neuter
n	-	neuter
n pl	-	neuter plural

pl	-	plural
v mod	-	modal verb
vi	-	intransitive verb
vi, vt	-	intransitive, transitive verb
vt	-	transitive verb

GERMAN
PHRASEBOOK

This section contains
important phrases that may
come in handy in various
real-life situations.
The phrasebook will help
you ask for directions, clarify
a price, buy tickets, and
order food at a restaurant

T&P Books Publishing

PHRASEBOOK
CONTENTS

T&P Books Publishing

Excuse me, ...	**Entschuldigen Sie bitte, ...** [ɛntˈʃʊldɪɡən ziː 'bɪtə, ...]
Hello.	**Hallo.** [haˈloː]
Thank you.	**Danke.** [daŋkə]
Good bye.	**Auf Wiedersehen.** [aʊf ˈviːdɐˌzeːən]
Yes.	**Ja.** [jaː]
No.	**Nein.** [naɪn]
I don't know.	**Ich weiß nicht.** [ɪç vaɪs nɪçt]
Where? | Where to? | When?	**Wo? | Wohin? | Wann?** [voː? | voˈhɪn? | van?]

I need ...	**Ich brauche ...** [ɪç ˈbʁaʊxə ...]
I want ...	**Ich möchte ...** [ɪç ˈmœçtə ...]
Do you have ...?	**Haben Sie ...?** [haːbən ziː ...?]
Is there a ... here?	**Gibt es hier ...?** [giːpt ɛs hiːɐ ...?]
May I ...?	**Kann ich ...?** [kan ɪç ...?]
..., please (polite request)	**Bitte** [bɪtə]

I'm looking for ...	**Ich suche ...** [ɪç ˈzuːxə ...]
the restroom	**Toilette** [toaˈlɛtə]
an ATM	**Geldautomat** [gɛltʔaʊtoˌmaːt]
a pharmacy (drugstore)	**Apotheke** [apoˈteːkə]
a hospital	**Krankenhaus** [kʁaŋkənˌhaʊs]
the police station	**Polizeistation** [poliˈtsaɪ·ʃtaˌtsjoːn]
the subway	**U-Bahn** [uːbaːn]

a taxi	**Taxi** [taksi]
the train station	**Bahnhof** [baːnˌhoːf]

My name is ...	**Ich heiße ...** [ɪç 'haɪsə ...]
What's your name?	**Wie heißen Sie?** [viː 'haɪsən ziː?]
Could you please help me?	**Helfen Sie mir bitte.** [hɛlfən ziː miːɐ 'bɪtə]
I've got a problem.	**Ich habe ein Problem.** [ɪç 'haːbə aɪn pʀo'bleːm]
I don't feel well.	**Mir ist schlecht.** [miːɐ ɪs ʃlɛçt]
Call an ambulance!	**Rufen Sie einen Krankenwagen!** [ʀuːfən ziː 'aɪnən 'kʀaŋkənˌvaːgən!]
May I make a call?	**Darf ich telefonieren?** [daʁf ɪç telefo'niːʀən?]

I'm sorry.	**Entschuldigung.** [ɛnt'ʃuldɪgʊŋ]
You're welcome.	**Keine Ursache.** [kaɪnə 'uːɐˌzaχə]

I, me	**ich** [ɪç]
you (inform.)	**du** [duː]
he	**er** [eːɐ]
she	**sie** [ziː]
they (masc.)	**sie** [ziː]
they (fem.)	**sie** [ziː]
we	**wir** [viːɐ]
you (pl)	**ihr** [iːɐ]
you (sg, form.)	**Sie** [ziː]

ENTRANCE	**EINGANG** [aɪnˌgaŋ]
EXIT	**AUSGANG** [aʊsˌgaŋ]
OUT OF ORDER	**AUßER BETRIEB** [ˌaʊsɐ bə'tʀiːp]
CLOSED	**GESCHLOSSEN** [gə'ʃlɔsən]

OPEN	**OFFEN** [ɔfən]
FOR WOMEN	**FÜR DAMEN** [fyːɐ 'damən]
FOR MEN	**FÜR HERREN** [fyːɐ 'hɛʁən]

Questions

Where?	**Wo?** [vo:?]
Where to?	**Wohin?** [vo'hɪn?]
Where from?	**Woher?** [vo'heːɐ?]
Why?	**Warum?** [va'ʀʊm?]
For what reason?	**Wozu?** [vo'tsu:?]
When?	**Wann?** [van?]

How long?	**Wie lange?** [vi: 'laŋə?]
At what time?	**Um wie viel Uhr?** [ʊm vi: fi:l u:ɐ?]
How much?	**Wie viel?** [vi: fi:l?]
Do you have ...?	**Haben Sie ...?** [ha:bən zi: ...?]
Where is ...?	**Wo befindet sich ...?** [vo: bə'fɪndət zɪç ...?]

What time is it?	**Wie spät ist es?** [vi: ʃpɛːt ist ɛs?]
May I make a call?	**Darf ich telefonieren?** [daʁf ɪç telefo'ni:ʀən?]
Who's there?	**Wer ist da?** [veːɐ ist da:?]
Can I smoke here?	**Darf ich hier rauchen?** [daʁf ɪç hi:ɐ 'ʀaʊχən?]
May I ...?	**Darf ich ...?** [daʁf ɪç ...?]

Needs

I'd like ...	**Ich hätte gerne ...** [ɪç 'hɛtə 'gɛʁnə ...]
I don't want ...	**Ich will nicht ...** [ɪç vɪl nɪçt ...]
I'm thirsty.	**Ich habe Durst.** [ɪç 'ha:bə duʁst]
I want to sleep.	**Ich möchte schlafen.** [ɪç 'mœçtə 'ʃla:fən]

I want ...	**Ich möchte ...** [ɪç 'mœçtə ...]
to wash up	**abwaschen** [ap'vaʃən]
to brush my teeth	**meine Zähne putzen** [maɪnə 'tsɛ:nə 'pʊtsən]
to rest a while	**eine Weile ausruhen** [aɪnə 'vaɪlə 'aʊsˌʁu:ən]
to change my clothes	**meine Kleidung wechseln** [maɪnə 'klaɪdʊŋ 'vɛksəln]

to go back to the hotel	**zurück ins Hotel gehen** [tsu'ʁʏk ɪns ho'tɛl 'ge:ən]
to buy ...	**... kaufen** [... 'kaʊfən]
to go to ...	**... gehen** [... 'ge:ən]
to visit ...	**... besuchen** [... bə'zuχən]
to meet with ...	**... treffen** [... 'tʁɛfən]
to make a call	**einen Anruf tätigen** [aɪnən 'anˌʁu:f 'tɛ:tɪgən]

I'm tired.	**Ich bin müde.** [ɪç bɪn 'my:də]
We are tired.	**Wir sind müde.** [vi:ɐ zɪnt 'my:də]
I'm cold.	**Mir ist kalt.** [mi:ɐ ɪs kalt]
I'm hot.	**Mir ist heiß.** [mi:ɐ ɪs haɪs]
I'm OK.	**Mir passt es.** [mi:ɐ past ɛs]

I need to make a call.

Ich muss telefonieren.
[ɪç mʊs telefo'niːʀən]

I need to go to the restroom.

Ich muss auf die Toilette.
[ɪç mʊs 'aʊf di toa'lɛtə]

I have to go.

Ich muss gehen.
[ɪç mʊs 'geːən]

I have to go now.

Ich muss jetzt gehen.
[ɪç mʊs jɛtst 'geːən]

Asking for directions

Excuse me, ...

Entschuldigen Sie bitte, ...
[ɛntˈʃʊldɪgən ziː ˈbɪtə, ...]

Where is ...?

Wo befindet sich ...?
[vo bəˈfɪndət zɪç ...?]

Which way is ...?

Welcher Weg ist ...?
[vɛlçɐ veːk ist ...?]

Could you help me, please?

Könnten Sie mir bitte helfen?
[kœntən ziː miːɐ ˈbɪtə ˈhɛlfən?]

I'm looking for ...

Ich suche ...
[ɪç ˈzuːχə ...]

I'm looking for the exit.

Ich suche den Ausgang.
[ɪç ˈzuːχə den ˈaʊsˌgaŋ]

I'm going to ...

Ich fahre nach ...
[ɪç ˈfaːʀə naːχ ...]

Am I going the right way to ...?

Gehe ich richtig nach ...?
[geːə ɪç ˈʀɪçtɪç naːχ ...?]

Is it far?

Ist es weit?
[ist ɛs vaɪt?]

Can I get there on foot?

Kann ich dort zu Fuß hingehen?
[kan ɪç dɔʁt tsu fuːs ˈhɪnˌgeːən?]

Can you show me on the map?

**Können Sie es mir auf
der Karte zeigen?**
[kœnən ziː ɛs miːɐ aʊf
deːɐ ˈkaʁtə ˈtsaɪgən?]

Show me where we are right now.

Zeigen Sie mir wo wir gerade sind.
[tsaɪgən ziː miːɐ vo: viːɐ gəˈʀaːdə zɪnt]

Here

Hier
[hiːɐ]

There

Dort
[dɔʁt]

This way

Hierher
[hiːɐˈheːɐ]

Turn right.

Biegen Sie rechts ab.
[biːgən ziː ʀɛçts ap]

Turn left.

Biegen Sie links ab.
[biːgən ziː lɪŋks ap]

first (second, third) turn

erste (zweite, dritte) Abzweigung
[ɛʁstə (ˈtsvaɪtə, ˈdʀɪtə) ˈapˌtsvaɪguŋ]

to the right

nach rechts
[naːχ ʀɛçts]

to the left

nach links
[na:χ lɪŋks]

Go straight ahead.

Laufen Sie geradeaus.
[laʊfən zi: gəʀa:də'ʔaʊs]

Signs

WELCOME!	**HERZLICH WILLKOMMEN!** [hɛʁtslɪç vɪl'kɔmən!]
ENTRANCE	**EINGANG** [aɪn‚gaŋ]
EXIT	**AUSGANG** [aʊs‚gaŋ]
PUSH	**DRÜCKEN** [dʁʏkən]
PULL	**ZIEHEN** [tsiːən]
OPEN	**OFFEN** [ɔfən]
CLOSED	**GESCHLOSSEN** [gə'ʃlɔsən]
FOR WOMEN	**FÜR DAMEN** [fyːɐ 'damən]
FOR MEN	**FÜR HERREN** [fyːɐ 'hɛʁən]
GENTLEMEN, GENTS	**HERREN-WC** [hɛʁən-veˈtseː]
WOMEN	**DAMEN-WC** [daːmən-veˈtseː]
DISCOUNTS	**RABATT | REDUZIERT** [ʁaˈbat | ʁeduˈtsiːɐt]
SALE	**AUSVERKAUF** [aʊsfɛɐ‚kaʊf]
FREE	**GRATIS** [gʁaːtɪs]
NEW!	**NEU!** [nɔɪ!]
ATTENTION!	**ACHTUNG!** [aχtʊŋ!]
NO VACANCIES	**KEINE ZIMMER FREI** [kaɪnə 'tsɪmɐ fʁaɪ]
RESERVED	**RESERVIERT** [ʁezɛʁ'viːɐt]
ADMINISTRATION	**VERWALTUNG** [fɛɐ'valtʊŋ]
STAFF ONLY	**NUR FÜR PERSONAL** [nuːɐ fyːɐ pɛʁzo'naːl]

BEWARE OF THE DOG! **BISSIGER HUND**
[bɪsɪgɐ hʊnt]

NO SMOKING! **RAUCHEN VERBOTEN**
[ʀaʊχən fɛɐˈboːtən]

DO NOT TOUCH! **NICHT ANFASSEN!**
[nɪçt 'anfasən!]

DANGEROUS **GEFÄHRLICH**
[gəˈfɛːɐlɪç]

DANGER **GEFAHR**
[gəˈfaːɐ]

HIGH VOLTAGE **HOCHSPANNUNG**
[hoːχˌʃpanʊŋ]

NO SWIMMING! **BADEN VERBOTEN**
[baːdən fɛɐˈboːtən]

OUT OF ORDER **AUßER BETRIEB**
[ˌaʊsɐ bəˈtʀiːp]

FLAMMABLE **LEICHTENTZÜNDLICH**
[laɪçt?ɛnˈtsʏntlɪç]

FORBIDDEN **VERBOTEN**
[fɛɐˈboːtən]

NO TRESPASSING! **DURCHGANG VERBOTEN**
[dʊʁçˌgaŋ fɛɐˈboːtən]

WET PAINT **FRISCH GESTRICHEN**
[fʀɪʃ gəˈʃtʀɪçən]

CLOSED FOR RENOVATIONS **WEGEN RENOVIERUNG GESCHLOSSEN**
[veːgən ʀenoˈviːʀʊŋ gəˈʃlɔsən]

WORKS AHEAD **ACHTUNG BAUARBEITEN**
[aχtʊŋ 'baʊ?aʁˌbaɪtən]

DETOUR **UMLEITUNG**
[ʊmˌlaɪtʊŋ]

Transportation. General phrases

plane	**Flugzeug** [fluːkˌtsɔɪk]
train	**Zug** [tsuːk]
bus	**Bus** [bʊs]
ferry	**Fähre** [fɛːʀə]
taxi	**Taxi** [taksi]
car	**Auto** [aʊto]

schedule	**Zeitplan** [tsaɪtˌplaːn]
Where can I see the schedule?	**Wo kann ich den Zeitplan sehen?** [voː kan ɪç den 'tsaɪtˌplaːn 'zeːən?]
workdays (weekdays)	**Arbeitstage** [aʀbaɪtsˌtaːgə]
weekends	**Wochenenden** [vɔχənˌʔɛndən]
holidays	**Ferien** [feːʀɪən]

DEPARTURE	**ABFLUG** [apfluːk]
ARRIVAL	**ANKUNFT** [ankʊnft]
DELAYED	**VERSPÄTET** [fɛɐ'ʃpɛːtət]
CANCELLED	**GESTRICHEN** [gə'ʃtʀɪçən]

next (train, etc.)	**nächster** [nɛːçstə]
first	**erster** [eːɐstə]
last	**letzter** [lɛtstə]

When is the next ...?	**Wann kommt der nächste ...?** [van kɔmt deːɐ 'nɛːçstə ...?]
When is the first ...?	**Wann kommt der erste ...?** [van kɔmt deːɐ 'eːɐstə ...?]

When is the last ...?

Wann kommt der letzte ...?
[van kɔmt deːɐ 'lɛtstə ...?]

transfer (change of trains, etc.)

Transfer
[tʀansˈfeːɐ]

to make a transfer

einen Transfer machen
[aɪnən tʀansˈfeːɐ 'maxən]

Do I need to make a transfer?

Muss ich einen Transfer machen?
[mʊs ɪç 'aɪnən tʀansˈfeːɐ 'maxən?]

Buying tickets

Where can I buy tickets?	**Wo kann ich Fahrkarten kaufen?** [vo: kan ɪç 'fa:ɐ̯ˌkaʁtən 'kaʊfən?]
ticket	**Fahrkarte** [fa:ɐ̯ˌkaʁtə]
to buy a ticket	**Eine Fahrkarte kaufen** [aɪnə 'fa:ɐ̯ˌkaʁtə 'kaʊfən]
ticket price	**Fahrpreis** [fa:ɐ̯ˌpʁaɪs]

Where to?	**Wohin?** [vo'hɪn?]
To what station?	**Welche Station?** [vɛlçə ʃta'tsjo:n?]
I need ...	**Ich brauche ...** [ɪç 'bʁaʊχə ...]
one ticket	**eine Fahrkarte** [aɪnə 'fa:ɐ̯ˌkaʁtə]
two tickets	**zwei Fahrkarten** [tsvaɪ 'fa:ɐ̯ˌkaʁtən]
three tickets	**drei Fahrkarten** [dʁaɪ 'fa:ɐ̯ˌkaʁtən]

one-way	**in eine Richtung** [ɪn 'aɪnə 'ʁɪçtʊŋ]
round-trip	**hin und zurück** [hɪn ʊnt tsu'ʁʏk]
first class	**erste Klasse** [ɛʁstə 'klasə]
second class	**zweite Klasse** [tsvaɪtə 'klasə]

today	**heute** [hɔɪtə]
tomorrow	**morgen** [mɔʁgən]
the day after tomorrow	**übermorgen** [y:bɐˌmɔʁgən]
in the morning	**am Vormittag** [am 'fo:ɐmɪta:k]
in the afternoon	**am Nachmittag** [am 'na:χmɪˌta:k]
in the evening	**am Abend** [am 'a:bənt]

aisle seat

Gangplatz
[gaŋˌplats]

window seat

Fensterplatz
[fɛnstɐˌplats]

How much?

Wie viel?
[vi: fi:l?]

Can I pay by credit card?

Kann ich mit Karte zahlen?
[kan ɪç mɪt ˈkaʁtə ˈtsa:lən?]

Bus

bus	**Bus** [bʊs]
intercity bus	**Fernbus** [fɛʁnbʊs]
bus stop	**Bushaltestelle** [bʊshaltəˌʃtɛlə]
Where's the nearest bus stop?	**Wo ist die nächste Bushaltestelle?** [vo: ist di 'nɛ:çstə 'bʊshaltəˌʃtɛlə?]
number (bus ~, etc.)	**Nummer** [nʊmə]
Which bus do I take to get to ...?	**Welchen Bus nehme ich um nach ... zu kommen?** [vɛlçən bʊs 'ne:mə ɪç um na:χ ... tsu 'kɔmən?]
Does this bus go to ...?	**Fährt dieser Bus nach ...?** [fɛ:ɐt 'di:zɐ bʊs na:χ ...?]
How frequent are the buses?	**Wie oft fahren die Busse?** [vi: ɔft 'fa:ʀən di 'bʊsə?]
every 15 minutes	**alle fünfzehn Minuten** [alə 'fʏnftse:n mi'nu:tən]
every half hour	**jede halbe Stunde** [je:də 'halbə 'ʃtʊndə]
every hour	**jede Stunde** [je:də 'ʃtʊndə]
several times a day	**mehrmals täglich** [me:ɐma:ls 'tɛ:klɪç]
... times a day	**... Mal am Tag** [... mal am ta:k]
schedule	**Zeitplan** [tsaɪtˌpla:n]
Where can I see the schedule?	**Wo kann ich den Zeitplan sehen?** [vo: kan ɪç den 'tsaɪtˌpla:n 'ze:ən?]
When is the next bus?	**Wann kommt der nächste Bus?** [van kɔmt de:ɐ 'nɛ:çstə bʊs?]
When is the first bus?	**Wann kommt der erste Bus?** [van kɔmt de:ɐ 'ɛʁstə bʊs?]
When is the last bus?	**Wann kommt der letzte Bus?** [van kɔmt de:ɐ 'lɛtstə bʊs?]

stop

Halt
[halt]

next stop

nächster Halt
[nɛ:çstə halt]

last stop (terminus)

letzter Halt
[lɛtstə halt]

Stop here, please.

Halten Sie hier bitte an.
[haltən zi: hi:ɐ 'bɪtə an]

Excuse me, this is my stop.

**Entschuldigen Sie mich,
dies ist meine Haltestelle.**
[ɛnt'ʃʊldɪgən zi: mɪç,
di:s ist maɪnə 'haltəʃtɛlə]

Train

train	**Zug** [tsuːk]
suburban train	**S-Bahn** [ɛsˌbaːn]
long-distance train	**Fernzug** [fɛʁnˌtsuːk]
train station	**Bahnhof** [baːnˌhoːf]
Excuse me, where is the exit to the platform?	**Entschuldigen Sie bitte, wo ist der Ausgang zum Bahngleis?** [ɛntˈʃʊldɪɡən ziː ˈbɪtə, voː ist deːɐ ˈaʊsɡaŋ tsʊm ˈbaːnˌɡlaɪs?]

Does this train go to ...?	**Fährt dieser Zug nach ...?** [fɛːɐt ˈdiːzɐ tsuːk naːχ ...?]
next train	**nächster Zug** [nɛːçstɐ tsuːk]
When is the next train?	**Wann kommt der nächste Zug?** [van kɔmt deːɐ ˈnɛːçstə tsuːk?]
Where can I see the schedule?	**Wo kann ich den Zeitplan sehen?** [voː kan ɪç den ˈtsaɪtˌplaːn ˈzeːən?]
From which platform?	**Von welchem Bahngleis?** [fɔn ˈvɛlçəm ˈbaːnˌɡlaɪs?]
When does the train arrive in ...?	**Wann kommt der Zug in ... an?** [van kɔmt deːɐ tsuːk ɪn ... an?]

Please help me.	**Helfen Sie mir bitte.** [hɛlfən ziː miːɐ ˈbɪtə]
I'm looking for my seat.	**Ich suche meinen Platz.** [ɪç ˈzuːχə ˈmaɪnen plats]
We're looking for our seats.	**Wir suchen unsere Plätze.** [viːɐ ˈzuːχən ˈʊnzərə ˈplɛtsə]

My seat is taken.	**Unser Platz ist besetzt.** [ʊnzɐ plats ist bəˈzɛtst]
Our seats are taken.	**Unsere Plätze sind besetzt.** [ʊnzərə ˈplɛtsə zɪnt bəˈzɛtst]
I'm sorry but this is my seat.	**Entschuldigen Sie, aber das ist mein Platz.** [ɛntˈʃʊldɪɡən ziː, ˈaːbɐ das ist maɪn plats]

Is this seat taken?

May I sit here?

Ist der Platz frei?
[ist deːɐ plats fʁaɪ?]

Darf ich mich hier setzen?
[daʁf ɪç mɪç hiːɐ 'zɛtsən?]

On the train. Dialogue (No ticket)

Ticket, please.
Fahrkarte bitte.
[faːɐ̯ˌkaʁtə bɪtə]

I don't have a ticket.
Ich habe keine Fahrkarte.
[ɪç ˈhaːbə kaɪnə ˈfaːɐ̯ˌkaʁtə]

I lost my ticket.
Ich habe meine Fahrkarte verloren.
[ɪç ˈhaːbə maɪnə ˈfaːɐ̯ˌkaʁtə fɛɐ̯ˈloːʁən]

I forgot my ticket at home.
Ich habe meine Fahrkarte zuhause vergessen.
[ɪç ˈhaːbə maɪnə ˈfaːɐ̯ˌkaʁtə tsuˈhaʊzə fɛɐ̯ˈgɛsən]

You can buy a ticket from me.
Sie können von mir eine Fahrkarte kaufen.
[ziː ˈkœnən fɔn miːɐ̯ ˈaɪnə ˈfaːɐ̯ˌkaʁtə ˈkaʊfən]

You will also have to pay a fine.
Sie werden auch eine Strafe zahlen.
[ziː ˈveːɐ̯dən aʊχ ˈaɪnə ˈʃtʁaːfə ˈtsaːlən]

Okay.
Gut.
[guːt]

Where are you going?
Wohin fahren Sie?
[voˈhɪn ˈfaːʁən ziː?]

I'm going to …
Ich fahre nach …
[ɪç ˈfaːʁə naːχ …]

How much? I don't understand.
Wie viel? Ich verstehe nicht.
[viː fiːl? ɪç fɛɐ̯ˈʃteːə nɪçt]

Write it down, please.
Schreiben Sie es bitte auf.
[ʃʁaɪbən ziː ɛs ˈbɪtə aʊf]

Okay. Can I pay with a credit card?
Gut. Kann ich mit Karte zahlen?
[guːt. kan ɪç mɪt ˈkaʁtə ˈtsaːlən?]

Yes, you can.
Ja, das können Sie.
[jaː, das ˈkœnən ziː]

Here's your receipt.
Hier ist ihre Quittung.
[hiːɐ̯ ist ˈiːʁə ˈkvɪtʊŋ]

Sorry about the fine.
Tut mir leid wegen der Strafe.
[tuːt miːɐ̯ laɪt ˈveːgən deːɐ̯ ˈʃtʁaːfə]

That's okay. It was my fault.
Das ist in Ordnung. Es ist meine Schuld.
[das is ɪn ˈɔʁdnʊŋ. ɛs ist ˈmaɪnə ʃʊlt]

Enjoy your trip.
Genießen Sie Ihre Fahrt.
[gəˈniːsən ziː ˈiːʁə faːɐ̯t]

Taxi

taxi	**Taxi** [taksi]
taxi driver	**Taxifahrer** [taksi͵faːʀɐ]
to catch a taxi	**Ein Taxi nehmen** [aɪn 'taksi 'neːmən]
taxi stand	**Taxistand** [taksi͵ʃtant]
Where can I get a taxi?	**Wo kann ich ein Taxi bekommen?** [voː kan ɪç aɪn 'taksi be'kɔmən?]
to call a taxi	**Ein Taxi rufen** [aɪn 'taksi 'ʀuːfən]
I need a taxi.	**Ich brauche ein Taxi.** [ɪç 'bʀaʊχə aɪn 'taksi]
Right now.	**Jetzt sofort.** [jɛtst zo'fɔʀt]
What is your address (location)?	**Wie ist Ihre Adresse?** [vi ist 'iːʀə a'dʀɛsə?]
My address is ...	**Meine Adresse ist ...** [maɪnə a'dʀɛsə ist ...]
Your destination?	**Ihr Ziel?** [iːɐ tsiːl?]
Excuse me, ...	**Entschuldigen Sie bitte, ...** [ɛnt'ʃʊldɪgən zi: 'bɪtə, ...]
Are you available?	**Sind Sie frei?** [zɪnt zi: fʀaɪ?]
How much is it to get to ...?	**Was kostet die Fahrt nach ...?** [vas 'koːstət di faːɐt naχ ...?]
Do you know where it is?	**Wissen Sie wo es ist?** [vɪsən zi: voː ɛs 'ist?]
Airport, please.	**Flughafen, bitte.** [fluːk͵haːfən, 'bɪtə]
Stop here, please.	**Halten Sie hier bitte an.** [haltən zi: hiːɐ 'bɪtə an]
It's not here.	**Das ist nicht hier.** [das is nɪçt hiːɐ]
This is the wrong address.	**Das ist die falsche Adresse.** [das is di: 'falʃə a'dʀɛsə]
Turn left.	**nach links** [naːχ lɪŋks]
Turn right.	**nach rechts** [naːχ ʀɛçts]

How much do I owe you?

Was schulde ich Ihnen?
[vas 'ʃʊldə ɪç 'iːnən?]

I'd like a receipt, please.

Ich würde gerne
ein Quittung haben, bitte.
[ɪç 'vʏʁdə 'gɛʁnə
aɪn 'kvɪtʊŋ 'haːbən, 'bɪtə]

Keep the change.

Stimmt so.
[ʃtɪmt zoː]

Would you please wait for me?

Warten Sie auf mich bitte.
[vaʁtən ziː 'aʊf mɪç 'bɪtə]

five minutes

fünf Minuten
[fʏnf miˈnuːtən]

ten minutes

zehn Minuten
[tseːn miˈnuːtən]

fifteen minutes

fünfzehn Minuten
[fʏnftseːn miˈnuːtən]

twenty minutes

zwanzig Minuten
[tsvantsɪç miˈnuːtən]

half an hour

eine halbe Stunde
[aɪnə 'halbə 'ʃtʊndə]

Hotel

Hello.	**Guten Tag.** [ˌɡuːtən 'taːk]
My name is …	**Mein Name ist …** [maɪn 'naːmə ist …]
I have a reservation.	**Ich habe eine Reservierung.** [ɪç 'haːbɛ 'aɪnə ʀezɛʀ'viːʀʊŋ]
I need …	**Ich brauche …** [ɪç 'bʀaʊχə …]
a single room	**ein Einzelzimmer** [aɪn 'aɪntsəlˌtsɪmɐ]
a double room	**ein Doppelzimmer** [aɪn 'dopəlˌtsɪmɐ]
How much is that?	**Wie viel kostet das?** [viː fiːl 'kɔstət das?]
That's a bit expensive.	**Das ist ein bisschen teuer.** [das is aɪn 'bɪsçən 'tɔɪɐ]
Do you have anything else?	**Haben Sie sonst noch etwas?** [haːbən ziː zɔnst nɔχ 'ɛtvas?]
I'll take it.	**Ich nehme es.** [ɪç 'neːmə ɛs]
I'll pay in cash.	**Ich zahle bar.** [ɪç 'tsaːlə baːɐ]
I've got a problem.	**Ich habe ein Problem.** [ɪç 'haːbə aɪn pʀo'bleːm]
My … is broken.	**… ist kaputt.** [… ɪst ka'pʊt]
My … is out of order.	**… ist außer Betrieb.** [… ɪst 'aʊsə bə'tʀiːp]
TV	**Mein Fernseher** [maɪn 'fɛʀnˌzeːɐ]
air conditioner	**Meine Klimaanlage** [maɪnə 'kliːmaˌʔanlaːɡə]
tap	**Mein Wasserhahn** [maɪn 'vasɐˌhaːn]
shower	**Meine Dusche** [maɪnə 'duːʃə]
sink	**Mein Waschbecken** [maɪn 'vaʃˌbɛkən]
safe	**Mein Tresor** [maɪn tʀe'zoːɐ]

door lock	**Mein Türschloss** [maɪn 'tyːʃlɔs]
electrical outlet	**Meine Steckdose** [maɪnə 'ʃtɛkˌdoːzə]
hairdryer	**Mein Föhn** [maɪn føːn]

I don't have ...	**Ich habe kein ...** [ɪç 'haːbə kaɪn ...]
water	**Wasser** [vasɐ]
light	**Licht** [lɪçt]
electricity	**Strom** [ʃtʁoːm]

Can you give me ...?	**Können Sie mir ... geben?** [kœnən ziː miːɐ ... 'geːbən?]
a towel	**ein Handtuch** [aɪn 'hantˌtuːχ]
a blanket	**eine Decke** [aɪnə 'dɛkə]
slippers	**Hausschuhe** [haʊsʃuːə]
a robe	**einen Bademantel** [aɪnən 'baːdəˌmantəl]
shampoo	**etwas Shampoo** [ɛtvas 'ʃampu]
soap	**etwas Seife** [ɛtvas 'zaɪfə]

I'd like to change rooms.	**Ich möchte ein anderes Zimmer haben.** [ɪç 'mœçtə aɪn 'andərəs 'tsɪmɐ 'haːbən]
I can't find my key.	**Ich kann meinen Schlüssel nicht finden.** [ɪç kan 'maɪnən 'ʃlʏsəl nɪçt 'fɪndən]
Could you open my room, please?	**Machen Sie bitte meine Tür auf.** ['maχən ziː 'bɪtə 'maɪnə tyːɐ 'aʊf]

Who's there?	**Wer ist da?** [veːɐ ist daː?]
Come in!	**Kommen Sie rein!** [kɔmən ziː ʁaɪn!]
Just a minute!	**Einen Moment bitte!** [aɪnən moˈmɛnt 'bɪtə!]
Not right now, please.	**Nicht jetzt bitte.** [nɪçt jɛtst 'bɪtə]
Come to my room, please.	**Kommen Sie bitte in mein Zimmer.** [kɔmən ziː 'bɪtə ɪn maɪn 'tsɪmɐ]

I'd like to order food service.

Ich würde gerne Essen bestellen.
[ɪç 'vʏʁdə 'gɛʁnə 'ɛsən bə'ʃtɛlən]

My room number is ...

Meine Zimmernummer ist ...
[maɪnə 'tsɪmə‚nʊmə ist ...]

I'm leaving ...

Ich reise ... ab.
[ɪç 'ʁaɪzə ... ap]

We're leaving ...

Wir reisen ... ab.
[viːɐ 'ʁaɪzən ... ap]

right now

jetzt
[jɛtst]

this afternoon

diesen Nachmittag
[diːzən 'naːχmɪ‚taːk]

tonight

heute Abend
[hɔɪtə 'aːbənt]

tomorrow

morgen
[mɔʁgən]

tomorrow morning

morgen früh
[mɔʁgən fʁyː]

tomorrow evening

morgen Abend
[mɔʁgən 'aːbənt]

the day after tomorrow

übermorgen
[yːbə‚mɔʁgən]

I'd like to pay.

Ich möchte die Zimmerrechnung begleichen.
[ɪç 'mœçtə di 'tsɪmə‚ʁɛçnʊŋ bə'glaɪçən]

Everything was wonderful.

Alles war wunderbar.
[aləs vaːɐ 'vʊndəbaːɐ]

Where can I get a taxi?

Wo kann ich ein Taxi bekommen?
[voː kan ɪç aɪn 'taksi be'kɔmən?]

Would you call a taxi for me, please?

Würden Sie bitte ein Taxi für mich holen?
[vʏʁdən ziː 'bɪtə aɪn 'taksi fyːɐ mɪç 'hoːlən?]

Restaurant

Can I look at the menu, please?
Könnte ich die Speisekarte sehen bitte?
[kœntə ɪç di 'ʃpaɪzəˌkaʁtə 'zeːən 'bɪtə?]

Table for one.
Tisch für einen.
[tɪʃ fyːə 'aɪnən]

There are two (three, four) of us.
Wir sind zu zweit (dritt, viert).
[viːə zɪnt tsu tsvaɪt (dʁɪt, fiːət)]

Smoking
Raucher
[ʁaʊχɐ]

No smoking
Nichtraucher
[nɪçtˌʁaʊχɐ]

Excuse me! (addressing a waiter)
Entschuldigen Sie mich!
[ɛnt'ʃʊldɪgən ziː mɪç!]

menu
Speisekarte
[ʃpaɪzəˌkaʁtə]

wine list
Weinkarte
[vaɪnˌkaʁtə]

The menu, please.
Die Speisekarte bitte.
[di 'ʃpaɪzəˌkaʁtə 'bɪtə]

Are you ready to order?
Sind Sie bereit zum bestellen?
[zɪnt ziː bəˈʁaɪt tsʊm bəˈʃtɛlən?]

What will you have?
Was würden Sie gerne haben?
[vas 'vyʁdən ziː 'gɛʁnə 'haːbən?]

I'll have …
Ich möchte …
[ɪç 'mœçtə …]

I'm a vegetarian.
Ich bin Vegetarier /Vegetarierin/.
[ɪç bɪn vegeˈtaːʁɪɐ /vegeˈtaːʁɪəʁɪn/]

meat
Fleisch
[flaɪʃ]

fish
Fisch
[fɪʃ]

vegetables
Gemüse
[gəˈmyːzə]

Do you have vegetarian dishes?
Haben Sie vegetarisches Essen?
[haːbən ziː vegeˈtaːʁɪʃəs 'ɛsən?]

I don't eat pork.
Ich esse kein Schweinefleisch.
[ɪç 'ɛsə kaɪn 'ʃvaɪnəˌflaɪʃ]

Band-Aid
Er /Sie/ isst kein Fleisch.
[eːɐ /ziː/ ist kaɪn flaɪʃ]

I am allergic to …
Ich bin allergisch auf …
[ɪç bɪn aˈlɛʁgɪʃ aʊf …]

Would you please bring me ...

Könnten Sie mir bitte ... bringen.
[kœntən zi: mi:ɐ 'bɪtə ... 'bʀɪŋən]

salt | pepper | sugar

Salz | Pfeffer | Zucker
[zalts | 'pfɛfɐ | 'tsʊkɐ]

coffee | tea | dessert

Kaffee | Tee | Nachtisch
[kafe | te: | 'na:χˌtɪʃ]

water | sparkling | plain

Wasser | Sprudel | stilles
[vasɐ | 'ʃpʀu:dəl | 'ʃtɪləs]

a spoon | fork | knife

einen Löffel | eine Gabel | ein Messer
[aɪnən 'lœfəl | 'aɪnə 'gabəl | aɪn 'mɛsɐ]

a plate | napkin

einen Teller | eine Serviette
[aɪnən 'tɛlɐ | 'aɪnə zɛʀ'vɪɛtə]

Enjoy your meal!

Guten Appetit!
[ˌgutən ˌʔapə'tit!]

One more, please.

Noch einen bitte.
[nɔχ 'aɪnən 'bɪtə]

It was very delicious.

Es war sehr lecker.
[ɛs va:ɐ ze:ɐ 'lɛkɐ]

---

check | change | tip

Scheck | Wechselgeld | Trinkgeld
[ʃɛk | 'vɛksəlˌgɛlt | 'tʀɪŋkˌgɛlt]

Check, please.
(Could I have the check, please?)

Zahlen bitte.
[tsa:lən 'bɪtə]

Can I pay by credit card?

Kann ich mit Karte zahlen?
[kan ɪç mɪt 'kaʀtə 'tsa:lən?]

I'm sorry, there's a mistake here.

Entschuldigen Sie, hier ist ein Fehler.
[ɛnt'ʃʊldɪgən zi:, hi:ɐ ist aɪn 'fe:lɐ]

Shopping

Can I help you?

Kann ich Ihnen behilflich sein?
[kan ɪç 'i:nən bə'hɪlflɪç zaɪn?]

Do you have ...?

Haben Sie ...?
[ha:bən zi: ...?]

I'm looking for ...

Ich suche ...
[ɪç 'zu:χə ...]

I need ...

Ich brauche ...
[ɪç 'bʀauχə ...]

I'm just looking.

Ich möchte nur schauen.
[ɪç 'mœçtə nu:ɐ 'ʃauən]

We're just looking.

Wir möchten nur schauen.
[vi:ɐ 'mœçtən nu:ɐ 'ʃauən]

I'll come back later.

**Ich komme später noch einmal
zurück.**
[ɪç 'komə 'ʃpɛ:tɐ noχ 'aɪnma:l
tsu'ʀʏk]

We'll come back later.

Wir kommen später vorbei.
[vi:ɐ 'komən 'ʃpɛ:tɐ fo:ɐ'baɪ]

discounts | sale

Rabatt | Ausverkauf
[ʀa'bat | 'ausfɛɐˌkauf]

Would you please show me ...

Zeigen Sie mir bitte ...
[tsaɪgən zi: mi:ɐ 'bɪtə ...]

Would you please give me ...

Geben Sie mir bitte ...
[ge:bən zi: mi:ɐ 'bɪtə ...]

Can I try it on?

Kann ich es anprobieren?
[kan ɪç ɛs 'anpʀoˌbi:ʀən?]

Excuse me, where's the fitting room?

**Entschuldigen Sie bitte,
wo ist die Anprobe?**
[ɛnt'ʃuldɪgən zi: 'bɪtə,
vo: ist di 'anpʀo:bə?]

Which color would you like?

Welche Farbe mögen Sie?
[vɛlçə 'faʀbə 'møgən zi:?]

size | length

Größe | Länge
[gʀø:sə | 'lɛŋə]

How does it fit?

Wie sitzt es?
[vi: zɪtst ɛs?]

How much is it?

Was kostet das?
[vas 'ko:stət das?]

That's too expensive.

Das ist zu teuer.
[das is tsu 'tɔɪɐ]

I'll take it.

Ich nehme es.
[ɪç 'neːmə ɛs]

Excuse me, where do I pay?

**Entschuldigen Sie bitte,
wo ist die Kasse?**
[ɛnt'ʃʊldɪgən ziː 'bɪtə,
voː ist di 'kasə?]

Will you pay in cash or credit card?

Zahlen Sie Bar oder mit Karte?
[tsaːlən ziː baːɐ̯ 'oːdɐ mɪt 'kaʁtə?]

In cash | with credit card

in Bar | mit Karte
[ɪn baːɐ̯ | mɪt 'kaʁtə]

Do you want the receipt?

Brauchen Sie die Quittung?
[bʁaʊ̯xən ziː di 'kvɪtʊŋ?]

Yes, please.

Ja, bitte.
[jaː, 'bɪtə]

No, it's OK.

Nein, es ist ok.
[naɪn, ɛs ist o'keː]

Thank you. Have a nice day!

Danke. Einen schönen Tag noch!
[daŋkə. 'aɪnən 'ʃøːnən 'tak nɔχ!]

In town

Excuse me, ...	**Entschuldigen Sie bitte, ...** [ɛnt'ʃʊldɪgən zi: 'bɪtə, ...]
I'm looking for ...	**Ich suche ...** [ɪç 'zu:χə ...]
the subway	**die U-Bahn** [di 'u:ba:n]
my hotel	**mein Hotel** [maɪn ho'tɛl]
the movie theater	**das Kino** [das 'ki:no]
a taxi stand	**den Taxistand** [den 'taksi̩ʃtant]

an ATM	**einen Geldautomat** [aɪnən 'gɛlt?aʊto̩ma:t]
a foreign exchange office	**eine Wechselstube** [aɪnə 'vɛksəlʃtu:bə]
an internet café	**ein Internetcafé** [aɪn 'ɪntɛnɛt·ka̩fe:]
... street	**die ... -Straße** [di ... 'ʃtʀa:sə]
this place	**diesen Ort** [di:zən ɔʁt]

Do you know where ... is?	**Wissen Sie, wo ... ist?** [vɪsən zi:, vo: ... 'ist?]
Which street is this?	**Wie heißt diese Straße?** [vi: haɪst 'di:zə 'ʃtʀa:sə?]
Show me where we are right now.	**Zeigen Sie mir wo wir gerade sind.** [tsaɪgən zi: mi:ɐ vo: vi:ɐ gə'ʀa:də zɪnt]
Can I get there on foot?	**Kann ich dort zu Fuß hingehen?** [kan ɪç dɔʁt tsu fu:s 'hɪn͵ge:ən?]
Do you have a map of the city?	**Haben Sie einen Stadtplan?** [ha:bən zi: 'aɪnən 'ʃtat͵pla:n?]

How much is a ticket to get in?	**Was kostet eine Eintrittskarte?** [vas 'ko:stət 'aɪnə 'aɪntʀɪts͵kaʁtə?]
Can I take pictures here?	**Darf man hier fotografieren?** [daʁf man hi:ɐ fotogʀa'fi:ʀən?]
Are you open?	**Haben Sie offen?** [ha:bən zi: 'ɔfən?]

When do you open?

Wann öffnen Sie?
[van 'œfnən ziː?]

When do you close?

Wann schließen Sie?
[van 'ʃliːsən ziː?]

Money

money	**Geld** [gɛlt]
cash	**Bargeld** [baːɐ̯ˌgɛlt]
paper money	**Papiergeld** [paˈpiːɐ̯ˌgɛlt]
loose change	**Kleingeld** [klaɪnˌgɛlt]
check | change | tip	**Scheck | Wechselgeld | Trinkgeld** [ʃɛk | ˈvɛksəlˌgɛlt | ˈtrɪŋkˌgɛlt]
credit card	**Kreditkarte** [kreˈdiːtˌkaʁtə]
wallet	**Geldbeutel** [gɛltˌbɔɪtəl]
to buy	**kaufen** [kaʊfən]
to pay	**zahlen** [tsaːlən]
fine	**Strafe** [ʃtʁaːfə]
free	**kostenlos** [kɔstənloːs]
Where can I buy ...?	**Wo kann ich ... kaufen?** [voː kan ɪç ... ˈkaʊfən?]
Is the bank open now?	**Ist die Bank jetzt offen?** [ist di baŋk jɛtst ˈɔfən?]
When does it open?	**Wann öffnet sie?** [van ˈœfnət ziː?]
When does it close?	**Wann schließt sie?** [van ʃliːst ziː?]
How much?	**Wie viel?** [viː fiːl?]
How much is this?	**Was kostet das?** [vas ˈkoːstət das?]
That's too expensive.	**Das ist zu teuer.** [das is tsu ˈtɔɪɐ]
Excuse me, where do I pay?	**Entschuldigen Sie bitte, wo ist die Kasse?** [ɛntˈʃuldɪgən ziː ˈbɪtə, voː ist di ˈkasə?]

Check, please.

Ich möchte zahlen.
[ɪç 'mœçtə 'tsaːlən]

Can I pay by credit card?

Kann ich mit Karte zahlen?
[kan ɪç mɪt 'kaʁtə 'tsaːlən?]

Is there an ATM here?

Gibt es hier einen Geldautomat?
[giːpt ɛs hiːɐ 'aɪnən 'gɛltʔautoˌmaːt?]

I'm looking for an ATM.

Ich brauche einen Geldautomat.
[ɪç 'bʁauxə 'aɪnən 'gɛltʔautoˌmaːt]

I'm looking for a foreign exchange office.

Ich suche eine Wechselstube.
[ɪç 'zuːxə 'aɪnə 'vɛksəlˌʃtuːbə]

I'd like to change ...

Ich möchte ... wechseln.
[ɪç 'mœçtə ... 'vɛksəln]

What is the exchange rate?

Was ist der Wechselkurs?
[vas ɪst deːɐ 'vɛksəlˌkuʁs?]

Do you need my passport?

Brauchen Sie meinen Reisepass?
[bʁauxən ziː 'maɪnən 'ʁaɪzəˌpas?]

Time

What time is it?	**Wie spät ist es?** [vi: ʃpɛ:t ist ɛs?]
When?	**Wann?** [van?]
At what time?	**Um wie viel Uhr?** [ʊm vifi:l u:ɐ?]
now | later | after …	**jetzt | später | nach …** [jɛtst | 'ʃpɛ:tɐ | na:χ …]
one o'clock	**ein Uhr** [aɪn u:ɐ]
one fifteen	**Viertel zwei** [fɪʁtəl tsvaɪ]
one thirty	**ein Uhr dreißig** [aɪn u:ɐ 'dʀaɪsɪç]
one forty-five	**Viertel vor zwei** [fɪʁtəl fo:ɐ tsvaɪ]
one | two | three	**eins | zwei | drei** [aɪns | tsvaɪ | dʀaɪ]
four | five | six	**vier | fünf | sechs** [fi:ɐ | fʏnf | zɛks]
seven | eight | nine	**sieben | acht | neun** [zi:bən | aχt | nɔɪn]
ten | eleven | twelve	**zehn | elf | zwölf** [tse:n | ɛlf | tsvœlf]
in …	**in …** [ɪn …]
five minutes	**fünf Minuten** [fʏnf mi'nu:tən]
ten minutes	**zehn Minuten** [tse:n mi'nu:tən]
fifteen minutes	**fünfzehn Minuten** [fʏnftse:n mi'nu:tən]
twenty minutes	**zwanzig Minuten** [tsvantsɪç mi'nu:tən]
half an hour	**einer halben Stunde** [aɪnɐ 'halbən 'ʃtʊndə]
an hour	**einer Stunde** [aɪnɐ 'ʃtʊndə]

in the morning	**am Vormittag** [am 'fo:emɪtaːk]
early in the morning	**früh am Morgen** [fʀy: am 'mɔʀgən]
this morning	**diesen Morgen** [diːzən 'mɔʀgən]
tomorrow morning	**morgen früh** [mɔʀgən fʀy:]

in the middle of the day	**am Mittag** [am 'mɪtaːk]
in the afternoon	**am Nachmittag** [am 'naːχmɪtaːk]
in the evening	**am Abend** [am 'aːbənt]
tonight	**heute Abend** [hɔɪtə 'aːbənt]

at night	**in der Nacht** [ɪn deːɐ naχt]
yesterday	**gestern** [gɛstən]
today	**heute** [hɔɪtə]
tomorrow	**morgen** [mɔʀgən]
the day after tomorrow	**übermorgen** [yːbə͜mɔʀgən]

What day is it today?	**Welcher Tag ist heute?** [vɛlçə taːk ist 'hɔɪtə?]
It's ...	**Es ist ...** [ɛs ist ...]
Monday	**Montag** [moːntaːk]
Tuesday	**Dienstag** [diːnstaːk]
Wednesday	**Mittwoch** [mɪtvɔχ]

Thursday	**Donnerstag** [dɔnɐstaːk]
Friday	**Freitag** [fʀaɪtaːk]
Saturday	**Samstag** [zamstaːk]
Sunday	**Sonntag** [zɔntaːk]

Greetings. Introductions

Hello. **Hallo.**
[ha'lo:]

Pleased to meet you. **Freut mich, Sie kennen zu lernen.**
[fʀɔɪt mɪç, zi: 'kɛnən tsu 'lɛʀnən]

Me too. **Ganz meinerseits.**
[gants 'maɪnɐ͜zaɪts]

I'd like you to meet ... **Darf ich vorstellen? Das ist ...**
[daʁf ɪç 'fo:ɐ͜ʃtɛlən? das ɪs ...]

Nice to meet you. **Sehr angenehm.**
[ze:ɐ 'angə͜ne:m]

How are you? **Wie geht es Ihnen?**
[vi: ge:t ɛs 'i:nən?]

My name is ... **Ich heiße ...**
[ɪç 'haɪsə ...]

His name is ... **Er heißt ...**
[e:ɐ haɪst ...]

Her name is ... **Sie heißt ...**
[zi: haɪst ...]

What's your name? **Wie heißen Sie?**
[vi: 'haɪsən zi:?]

What's his name? **Wie heißt er?**
[vi: haɪst e:ɐ?]

What's her name? **Wie heißt sie?**
[vi: haɪst zi:?]

What's your last name? **Wie ist Ihr Nachname?**
[vi: ɪst i:ɐ 'na:χ͜na:mə?]

You can call me ... **Sie können mich ... nennen.**
[zi: 'kœnən mɪç ... 'nɛnən]

Where are you from? **Woher kommen Sie?**
[vo'he:ɐ 'kɔmən zi:?]

I'm from ... **Ich komme aus ...**
[ɪç 'kɔmə 'aʊs ...]

What do you do for a living? **Was machen Sie beruflich?**
[vas 'maχən zi: bə'ʀu:flɪç?]

Who is this? **Wer ist das?**
[ve:ɐ ɪst das?]

Who is he? **Wer ist er?**
[ve:ɐ ɪst e:ɐ?]

Who is she? **Wer ist sie?**
[ve:ɐ ɪst zi:?]

Who are they? **Wer sind sie?**
[ve:ɐ zɪnt zi:?]

This is ...

Das ist ...
[das is ...]

my friend (masc.)

mein Freund
[maɪn frɔɪnt]

my friend (fem.)

meine Freundin
[maɪnə 'frɔɪndin]

my husband

mein Mann
[maɪn man]

my wife

meine Frau
[maɪnə 'fraʊ]

my father

mein Vater
[maɪn 'faːtə]

my mother

meine Mutter
[maɪnə 'mʊtə]

my brother

mein Bruder
[maɪn 'bʀuːdə]

my sister

meine Schwester
[maɪnə 'ʃvɛstə]

my son

mein Sohn
[maɪn zoːn]

my daughter

meine Tochter
[maɪnə 'tɔxtə]

This is our son.

Das ist unser Sohn.
[das is 'ʊnzɐ zoːn]

This is our daughter.

Das ist unsere Tochter.
[das is 'ʊnzərə 'tɔxtə]

These are my children.

Das sind meine Kinder.
[das zɪnt 'maɪnə 'kɪndə]

These are our children.

Das sind unsere Kinder.
[das zɪnt 'ʊnzərə 'kɪndə]

Farewells

Good bye!	**Auf Wiedersehen!** [aʊf 'viːdəˌzeːən!]
Bye! (inform.)	**Tschüs!** [ʧyːs!]
See you tomorrow.	**Bis morgen.** [bɪs 'mɔʁgən]
See you soon.	**Bis bald.** [bɪs balt]
See you at seven.	**Bis um sieben.** [bɪs ʊm ziːbən]

Have fun!	**Viel Spaß!** [fiːl ʃpaːs!]
Talk to you later.	**Wir sprechen später.** [viːɐ 'ʃpʁɛçən 'ʃpɛːtə]
Have a nice weekend.	**Ich wünsche Ihnen ein schönes Wochenende.** [ɪç 'vʏnʃə 'iːnən aɪn 'ʃøːnəs 'vɔχən ʔɛndə]
Good night.	**Gute Nacht.** [guːtə naχt]

It's time for me to go.	**Es ist Zeit, dass ich gehe.** [ɛs ist tsaɪt, das ɪç 'geːə]
I have to go.	**Ich muss gehen.** [ɪç mʊs 'geːən]
I will be right back.	**Ich bin gleich wieder da.** [ɪç bɪn glaɪç 'viːdə da]

It's late.	**Es ist schon spät.** [ɛs ist ʃoːn ʃpɛːt]
I have to get up early.	**Ich muss früh aufstehen.** [ɪç mʊs fʁyː 'aʊfˌʃteːən]
I'm leaving tomorrow.	**Ich reise morgen ab.** [ɪç 'ʁaɪzə 'mɔʁgən ap]
We're leaving tomorrow.	**Wir reisen morgen ab.** [viːɐ 'ʁaɪzən 'mɔʁgən ap]

Have a nice trip!	**Ich wünsche Ihnen eine gute Reise!** [ɪç 'vʏnʃə 'iːnən 'aɪnə 'guːtə 'ʁaɪzə!]
It was nice meeting you.	**Hat mich gefreut, Sie kennen zu lernen.** [hat mɪç gə'fʁɔɪt, ziː 'kɛnən tsu 'lɛʁnən]

It was nice talking to you.

**Hat mich gefreut mit Ihnen
zu sprechen.**
[hat mɪç gə'frɔɪt mɪt 'iːnən
tsu 'ʃprɛçən]

Thanks for everything.

Danke für alles.
[daŋkə fyːɐ 'aləs]

I had a very good time.

Ich hatte eine sehr gute Zeit.
[ɪç hatə 'aɪnə zeːɐ 'guːtə tsaɪt]

We had a very good time.

Wir hatten eine sehr gute Zeit.
[viːɐ 'hatən 'aɪnə zeːɐ 'guːtə tsaɪt]

It was really great.

Es war wirklich toll.
[ɛs vaːɐ 'vɪʁklɪç tɔl]

I'm going to miss you.

Ich werde Sie vermissen.
[ɪç 'veːɐdə ziː fɛɐ'mɪsən]

We're going to miss you.

Wir werden Sie vermissen.
[viːɐ 'veːɐdən ziː fɛɐ'mɪsən]

Good luck!

Viel Glück!
[fiːl glʏk!]

Say hi to ...

Grüßen Sie ...
[gʁyːsən ziː ...]

Foreign language

I don't understand.	**Ich verstehe nicht.** [ɪç fɛɐ'ʃteːə nɪçt]
Write it down, please.	**Schreiben Sie es bitte auf.** [ʃʀaɪbən ziː ɛs 'bɪtə aʊf]
Do you speak ...?	**Sprechen Sie ...?** [ʃpʀɛçən ziː ...?]

I speak a little bit of ...	**Ich spreche ein bisschen ...** [ɪç 'ʃpʀɛçə aɪn 'bɪsçən ...]
English	**Englisch** [ɛŋlɪʃ]
Turkish	**Türkisch** [tʏʁkɪʃ]
Arabic	**Arabisch** [a'ʀaːbɪʃ]
French	**Französisch** [fʀan'tsøːzɪʃ]

German	**Deutsch** [dɔɪtʃ]
Italian	**Italienisch** [ˌita'lɪeːnɪʃ]
Spanish	**Spanisch** [ʃpaːnɪʃ]
Portuguese	**Portugiesisch** [pɔʁtu'giːzɪʃ]
Chinese	**Chinesisch** [çi'neːzɪʃ]
Japanese	**Japanisch** [ja'paːnɪʃ]

Can you repeat that, please.	**Können Sie das bitte wiederholen.** [kœnən ziː das 'bɪtə viːdɐ'hoːlən]
I understand.	**Ich verstehe.** [ɪç fɛɐ'ʃteːə]
I don't understand.	**Ich verstehe nicht.** [ɪç fɛɐ'ʃteːə nɪçt]
Please speak more slowly.	**Sprechen Sie etwas langsamer.** [ʃpʀɛçən ziː 'ɛtvas 'laŋˌzaːmɐ]

Is that correct? (Am I saying it right?)	**Ist das richtig?** [ist das 'ʀɪçtɪç?]
What is this? (What does this mean?)	**Was ist das?** [vas ɪst das?]

Apologies

Excuse me, please.	**Entschuldigen Sie bitte.** [ɛntˈʃʊldɪgən ziː ˈbɪtə]
I'm sorry.	**Es tut mir leid.** [ɛs tuːt miːɐ laɪt]
I'm really sorry.	**Es tut mir sehr leid.** [ɛs tuːt miːɐ zeːɐ laɪt]
Sorry, it's my fault.	**Es tut mir leid, das ist meine Schuld.** [ɛs tuːt miːɐ laɪt, das ist ˈmaɪnə ʃʊlt]
My mistake.	**Das ist mein Fehler.** [das is maɪn ˈfeːlɐ]

May I ...?	**Darf ich ...?** [daʁf ɪç ...?]
Do you mind if I ...?	**Haben Sie etwas dagegen, wenn ich ...?** [haːbən ziː ˈɛtvas daˈgeːgən, vɛn ɪç ...?]
It's OK.	**Es ist okay.** [ɛs ist oˈkeː]
It's all right.	**Alles in Ordnung.** [aləs ɪn ˈɔʁdnʊŋ]
Don't worry about it.	**Machen Sie sich keine Sorgen.** [ˈmaxən ziː zɪç ˈkaɪnə ˈzɔʁgən]

Agreement

Yes.	**Ja.** [ja:]
Yes, sure.	**Ja, natürlich.** [ja:, na'ty:ɐlɪç]
OK (Good!)	**Ok! Gut!** [o'ke:! gu:t!]
Very well.	**Sehr gut.** [ze:ɐ gu:t]
Certainly!	**Natürlich!** [na'ty:ɐlɪç!]
I agree.	**Genau.** [ge'naʊ]

That's correct.	**Das stimmt.** [das ʃtɪmt]
That's right.	**Das ist richtig.** [das is 'ʀɪçtɪç]
You're right.	**Sie haben Recht.** [zi: 'ha:bən ʀɛçt]
I don't mind.	**Ich habe nichts dagegen.** [ɪç 'ha:bə nɪçts da'ge:gən]
Absolutely right.	**Völlig richtig.** [fœlɪç 'ʀɪçtɪç]

It's possible.	**Das kann sein.** [das kan zaɪn]
That's a good idea.	**Das ist eine gute Idee.** [das is 'aɪnə 'gu:tə i'de:]
I can't say no.	**Ich kann es nicht ablehnen.** [ɪç kan ɛs nɪçt 'ap‚le:nən]
I'd be happy to.	**Ich würde mich freuen.** [ɪç 'vʏʀdə mɪç 'fʀɔɪən]
With pleasure.	**Gerne.** [gɛʀnə]

Refusal. Expressing doubt

No.
Nein.
[naɪn]

Certainly not.
Natürlich nicht.
[na'ty:ɐlɪç nɪçt]

I don't agree.
Ich stimme nicht zu.
[ɪç 'ʃtɪmə nɪçt tsu]

I don't think so.
Das glaube ich nicht.
[das 'glaʊbə ɪç nɪçt]

It's not true.
Das ist falsch.
[das is falʃ]

You are wrong.
Sie liegen falsch.
[zi: 'li:gən falʃ]

I think you are wrong.
Ich glaube, Sie haben Unrecht.
[ɪç 'glaʊbə, zi: 'ha:bən 'ʊnˌʀɛçt]

I'm not sure.
Ich bin nicht sicher.
[ɪç bɪn nɪçt 'zɪçɐ]

It's impossible.
Das ist unmöglich.
[das is 'ʊnmø:klɪç]

Nothing of the kind (sort)!
Nichts dergleichen!
[nɪçts de:ɐ'glaɪçən!]

The exact opposite.
Im Gegenteil!
[ɪm 'ge:gəntaɪl!]

I'm against it.
Ich bin dagegen.
[ɪç bɪn da'ge:gən]

I don't care.
Es ist mir egal.
[ɛs ist mi:ɐ e'ga:l]

I have no idea.
Keine Ahnung.
[kaɪnə 'a:nʊŋ]

I doubt it.
Ich bezweifle, dass es so ist.
[ɪç bə'tsvaɪflə, das ɛs zo: ist]

Sorry, I can't.
Es tut mir leid, ich kann nicht.
[ɛs tu:t mi:ɐ laɪt, ɪç kan nɪçt]

Sorry, I don't want to.
Es tut mir leid, ich möchte nicht.
[ɛs tu:t mi:ɐ laɪt, ɪç 'mœçtə nɪçt]

Thank you, but I don't need this.
Danke, das brauche ich nicht.
[daŋkə, das 'bʀaʊχə ɪç nɪçt]

It's getting late.
Es ist schon spät.
[ɛs ist ʃo:n ʃpɛ:t]

I have to get up early.

Ich muss früh aufstehen.
[ɪç mʊs fʀyː 'aʊfˌʃteːən]

I don't feel well.

Mir geht es schlecht.
[miːɐ geːt ɛs ʃlɛçt]

Expressing gratitude

Thank you.

Danke.
[daŋkə]

Thank you very much.

Dankeschön.
[daŋkəʃøːn]

I really appreciate it.

Ich bin Ihnen sehr verbunden.
[ɪç bɪn 'iːnən zeːɐ ˌfɛɐ'bʊndən]

I'm really grateful to you.

Ich bin Ihnen sehr dankbar.
[ɪç bɪn 'iːnən zeːɐ 'daŋkbaːɐ]

We are really grateful to you.

Wir sind Ihnen sehr dankbar.
[viːɐ zɪnt 'iːnən zeːɐ 'daŋkbaːɐ]

Thank you for your time.

**Danke, dass Sie Ihre Zeit
geopfert haben.**
[daŋkə, das ziː 'iːʀə tsaɪt
gə'ʔɔpfet 'haːbən]

Thanks for everything.

Danke für alles.
[daŋkə fyːɐ 'aləs]

Thank you for ...

Danke für ...
[daŋkə fyːɐ ...]

your help

Ihre Hilfe
[iːʀə 'hɪlfə]

a nice time

die schöne Zeit
[di 'ʃøːnə tsaɪt]

a wonderful meal

das wunderbare Essen
[das 'vʊndebaːʀə 'ɛsən]

a pleasant evening

den angenehmen Abend
[den 'angəˌneːmən 'aːbənt]

a wonderful day

den wunderschönen Tag
[dɛn ˌvʊndeˈʃøːnən taːk]

an amazing journey

die interessante Führung
[di ɪntəʀɛ'santə 'fyːʀʊŋ]

Don't mention it.

Keine Ursache.
[kaɪnə 'uːɐˌzaxə]

You are welcome.

Nichts zu danken.
[nɪçts tsu 'daŋkən]

Any time.

Immer gerne.
[ɪmɐ 'gɛʀnə]

My pleasure.

Es freut mich, geholfen zu haben.
[ɛs fʀɔɪt mɪç, gə'hɔlfən tsu 'haːbən]

Forget it.

Vergessen Sie es.
[fɛɐ̯'gɛsən zi: ɛs]

Don't worry about it.

Machen Sie sich keine Sorgen.
['maxən zi: zɪç 'kaɪnə 'zɔʁgən]

Congratulations. Best wishes

Congratulations!	**Glückwunsch!** [glʏkˌvunʃ!]
Happy birthday!	**Alles gute zum Geburtstag!** [aləs ˈguːtə tsum gəˈbuʁtsˌtaːk!]
Merry Christmas!	**Frohe Weihnachten!** [ˌfʁoːə ˈvaɪnaχtən!]
Happy New Year!	**Frohes neues Jahr!** [ˌfʁoːəs ˈnɔɪəs jaːɐ!]

Happy Easter!	**Frohe Ostern!** [ˌfʁoːə ˈoːstən!]
Happy Hanukkah!	**Frohes Hanukkah!** [ˌfʁoːəs ˈhaːnuka:!]

I'd like to propose a toast.	**Ich möchte einen Toast ausbringen.** [ɪç ˈmœçtə ˈaɪnən toːst ˈausˌbʁɪŋən]
Cheers!	**Auf Ihr Wohl!** [auf iːɐ voːl!]
Let's drink to …!	**Trinken wir auf …!** [tʁɪŋkən viːɐ ˈauf …!]
To our success!	**Auf unseren Erfolg!** [auf ˈunzəʁən ɛɐˈfolk!]
To your success!	**Auf Ihren Erfolg!** [auf ˈiːʁən ɛɐˈfolk!]

Good luck!	**Viel Glück!** [fiːl glʏk!]
Have a nice day!	**Einen schönen Tag noch!** [aɪnən ˈʃøːnən taːk nɔχ!]
Have a good holiday!	**Haben Sie einen guten Urlaub!** [haːbən ziː ˈaɪnən ˈguːtən ˈuːɐˌlaup!]
Have a safe journey!	**Haben Sie eine sichere Reise!** [haːbən ziː ˈaɪnə ˈzɪçəʁə ˈʁaɪzə!]
I hope you get better soon!	**Ich hoffe es geht Ihnen bald besser!** [ɪç ˈhɔfə ɛs geːt ˈiːnən balt ˈbɛsə!]

Socializing

Why are you sad?	**Warum sind Sie traurig?** [va'ʀʊm zɪnt zi: 'tʀaʊʀɪç?]
Smile! Cheer up!	**Lächeln Sie!** [lɛçəln zi:!]
Are you free tonight?	**Sind Sie heute Abend frei?** [zɪnt zi: 'hɔɪtə 'a:bənt fʀaɪ?]
May I offer you a drink?	**Darf ich ihnen was zum Trinken anbieten?** [daʀf ɪç 'i:nən vas tsʊm 'tʀɪŋkən 'an,bi:tən?]
Would you like to dance?	**Möchten Sie tanzen?** [mœçtən zi: 'tantsən?]
Let's go to the movies.	**Gehen wir ins Kino.** [ge:ən vi:ɐ ɪns 'ki:no]
May I invite you to ...?	**Darf ich Sie ins ... einladen?** [daʀf ɪç zi: ɪns ... 'aɪn,la:dən?]
a restaurant	**Restaurant** [ʀɛsto'ʀaŋ]
the movies	**Kino** [ki:no]
the theater	**Theater** [te'a:tɐ]
go for a walk	**auf einen Spaziergang** [aʊf 'aɪnən ʃpa'tsi:ɐ,gaŋ]
At what time?	**Um wie viel Uhr?** [ʊm vifi:l u:ɐ?]
tonight	**heute Abend** [hɔɪtə 'a:bənt]
at six	**um sechs Uhr** [ʊm zɛks u:ɐ]
at seven	**um sieben Uhr** [ʊm 'zi:bən u:ɐ]
at eight	**um acht Uhr** [ʊm aχt u:ɐ]
at nine	**um neun Uhr** [ʊm 'nɔɪn u:ɐ]
Do you like it here?	**Gefällt es Ihnen hier?** [gə'fɛlt ɛs 'i:nən hi:ɐ?]
Are you here with someone?	**Sind Sie hier mit jemandem?** [zɪnt zi: hi:ɐ mɪt 'je:mandəm?]

I'm with my friend.

Ich bin mit meinem Freund.
[ɪç bɪn mɪt 'maɪnəm fʀɔɪnt]

I'm with my friends.

Ich bin mit meinen Freunden.
[ɪç bɪn mɪt 'maɪnəm 'fʀɔɪndən]

No, I'm alone.

Nein, ich bin alleine.
[naɪn, ɪç bɪn a'laɪnə]

Do you have a boyfriend?

Hast du einen Freund?
[hast du 'aɪnən fʀɔɪnt?]

I have a boyfriend.

Ich habe einen Freund.
[ɪç 'ha:bə 'aɪnən fʀɔɪnt]

Do you have a girlfriend?

Hast du eine Freundin?
[hast du 'aɪnə 'fʀɔɪndɪn?]

I have a girlfriend.

Ich habe eine Freundin.
[ɪç 'ha:bə 'aɪnə 'fʀɔɪndɪn]

Can I see you again?

Kann ich dich nochmals sehen?
[kan ɪç dɪç 'nɔχma:ls 'ze:ən?]

Can I call you?

Kann ich dich anrufen?
[kan ɪç dɪç 'an͜ʀu:fən?]

Call me. (Give me a call.)

Ruf mich an.
[ʀu:f mɪç an]

What's your number?

Was ist deine Nummer?
[vas ɪst 'daɪnə 'nʊmɐ?]

I miss you.

Ich vermisse dich.
[ɪç fɛɛ'mɪsə dɪç]

You have a beautiful name.

Sie haben einen schönen Namen.
[zi: 'ha:bən 'aɪnən 'ʃø:nən 'na:mən]

I love you.

Ich liebe dich.
[ɪç 'li:bə dɪç]

Will you marry me?

Willst du mich heiraten?
[vɪlst du mɪç 'haɪʀa:tən?]

You're kidding!

Sie machen Scherze!
[zi: 'maχən 'ʃɛʀtsə!]

I'm just kidding.

Ich habe nur gescherzt.
[ɪç 'ha:bə nu:ɐ gə'ʃɛʀtst]

Are you serious?

Ist das Ihr Ernst?
[ist das i:ɐ ɛʀnst?]

I'm serious.

Das ist mein Ernst.
[das is maɪn ɛʀnst]

Really?!

Echt?!
[ɛçt?!]

It's unbelievable!

Das ist unglaublich!
[das is ʊn'glaʊplɪç!]

I don't believe you.

Ich glaube Ihnen nicht.
[ɪç 'glaʊbə 'i:nən nɪçt]

I can't.

Ich kann nicht.
[ɪç kan nɪçt]

I don't know.

Ich weiß nicht.
[ɪç vaɪs nɪçt]

I don't understand you.

Ich verstehe Sie nicht.
[ɪç fɛɐ'ʃte:ə zi: nɪçt]

Please go away.

Bitte gehen Sie weg.
[bɪtə 'ge:ən zi: vɛk]

Leave me alone!

Lassen Sie mich in Ruhe!
[lasən zi: mɪç ɪn 'ʀu:ə!]

I can't stand him.

Ich kann ihn nicht ausstehen.
[ɪç kan i:n nɪçt 'aʊsˌʃte:ən]

You are disgusting!

Sie sind widerlich!
[zi: zɪnt 'vi:dɐlɪç!]

I'll call the police!

Ich rufe die Polizei an!
[ɪç 'ʀu:fə di ˌpoli'tsaɪ an!]

Sharing impressions. Emotions

I like it.	**Das gefällt mir.** [das gə'fɛlt miːɐ]
Very nice.	**Sehr nett.** [zeːɐ nɛt]
That's great!	**Das ist toll!** [das is tɔl!]
It's not bad.	**Das ist nicht schlecht.** [das is nɪçt ʃlɛçt]

I don't like it.	**Das gefällt mir nicht.** [das gə'fɛlt miːɐ nɪçt]
It's not good.	**Das ist nicht gut.** [das is nɪçt guːt]
It's bad.	**Das ist schlecht.** [das is ʃlɛçt]
It's very bad.	**Das ist sehr schlecht.** [das is zeːɐ ʃlɛçt]
It's disgusting.	**Das ist widerlich.** [das is 'viːdɐlɪç]

I'm happy.	**Ich bin glücklich.** [ɪç bɪn 'glʏklɪç]
I'm content.	**Ich bin zufrieden.** [ɪç bɪn tsu'fʀiːdən]
I'm in love.	**Ich bin verliebt.** [ɪç bɪn fɛɐ'liːpt]
I'm calm.	**Ich bin ruhig.** [ɪç bɪn 'ʀuːɪç]
I'm bored.	**Ich bin gelangweilt.** [ɪç bɪn gə'laŋˌvaɪlt]

I'm tired.	**Ich bin müde.** [ɪç bɪn 'myːdə]
I'm sad.	**Ich bin traurig.** [ɪç bɪn 'tʀaʊʀɪç]

I'm frightened.	**Ich habe Angst.** [ɪç 'haːbə aŋst]
I'm angry.	**Ich bin wütend.** [ɪç bɪn 'vyːtənt]
I'm worried.	**Ich mache mir Sorgen.** [ɪç 'maxə miːɐ 'zɔʀgən]
I'm nervous.	**Ich bin nervös.** [ɪç bɪn nɛʀ'vøːs]

I'm jealous. (envious)

Ich bin eifersüchtig.
[ɪç bɪn 'aɪfɐˌzʏçtɪç]

I'm surprised.

Ich bin überrascht.
[ɪç bɪn yːbɐ'ʀaʃt]

I'm perplexed.

Es ist mir peinlich.
[ɛs ist miːɐ 'paɪnˌlɪç]

Problems. Accidents

I've got a problem.
Ich habe ein Problem.
[ɪç 'haːbə aɪn pʀoˈbleːm]

We've got a problem.
Wir haben Probleme.
[viːɐ 'haːbən pʀoˈbleːmə]

I'm lost.
Ich bin verloren.
[ɪç bɪn fɛɐˈloːʀən]

I missed the last bus (train).
Ich habe den letzten Bus (Zug) verpasst.
[ɪç 'haːbə den 'lɛtstən bʊs (tsuːk) fɛɐˈpast]

I don't have any money left.
Ich habe kein Geld mehr.
[ɪç 'haːbə kaɪn gɛlt meːɐ]

I've lost my ...
Ich habe mein ... verloren.
[ɪç 'haːbə maɪn ... fɛɐˈloːʀən]

Someone stole my ...
Jemand hat mein ... gestohlen.
[jeːmant hat maɪn ... gəˈʃtoːlən]

passport
Reisepass
[ʀaɪzə‚pas]

wallet
Geldbeutel
[gɛlt‚bɔɪtəl]

papers
Papiere
[paˈpiːʀə]

ticket
Fahrkarte
[faːɐ‚kaʀtə]

money
Geld
[gɛlt]

handbag
Tasche
[taʃə]

camera
Kamera
[kameʀa]

laptop
Laptop
[lɛptɔp]

tablet computer
Tabletcomputer
[tɛblət·kɔm‚pjuːtɐ]

mobile phone
Handy
[hɛndi]

Help me!
Hilfe!
[hɪlfə!]

What's happened?
Was ist passiert?
[vas ɪst paˈsiːɐt?]

fire
Feuer
[fɔɪɐ]

shooting	**Schießerei** [ʃiːsəˈʀaɪ]
murder	**Mord** [mɔʁt]
explosion	**Explosion** [ɛksploˈzjoːn]
fight	**Schlägerei** [ʃlɛːgəˈʀaɪ]

Call the police!	**Rufen Sie die Polizei!** [ʀuːfən ziː di ˌpoliˈtsaɪ!]
Please hurry up!	**Schneller bitte!** [ʃnɛlɐ ˈbɪtə!]
I'm looking for the police station.	**Ich suche nach einer Polizeistation.** [ɪç ˈzuːχə naːχ ˈaɪnə poliˈtsaɪʃtaˌtsjoːn]
I need to make a call.	**Ich muss einen Anruf tätigen.** [ɪç mʊs ˈaɪnən ˈanˌʀuːf ˈtɛːtɪgən]
May I use your phone?	**Kann ich Ihr Telefon benutzen?** [kan ɪç iːɐ teleˈfoːn bəˈnʊtsən?]

I've been ...	**Ich wurde ...** [ɪç ˈvʏʁdə ...]
mugged	**ausgeraubt** [aʊsgəˌʀaʊpt]
robbed	**überfallen** [ˌyːbɐˈfalən]
raped	**vergewaltigt** [fɛɐgəˈvaltɪçt]
attacked (beaten up)	**angegriffen** [angəˌgʀɪfən]

Are you all right?	**Ist bei Ihnen alles in Ordnung?** [ist baɪ ˈiːnən ˈaləs ɪn ˈɔʁdnʊŋ?]
Did you see who it was?	**Haben Sie gesehen wer es war?** [haːbən ziː geˈzeːən veːɐ ɛs vaːɐ?]
Would you be able to recognize the person?	**Sind Sie in der Lage die Person wiederzuerkennen?** [zɪnt ziː ɪn deːɐ laːgə di pɛʁˈzoːn ˈviːdɛtsuʔɛɐˌkɛnən?]
Are you sure?	**Sind sie sicher?** [zɪnt ziː ˈzɪçɐ?]

Please calm down.	**Beruhigen Sie sich bitte!** [bəˈʀuːɪgən ziː zɪç ˈbɪtə!]
Take it easy!	**Ruhig!** [ʀuːɪç!]
Don't worry!	**Machen Sie sich keine Sorgen.** [maχən ziː zɪç ˈkaɪnə ˈzɔʁgən]
Everything will be fine.	**Alles wird gut.** [aləs vɪʁt guːt]
Everything's all right.	**Alles ist in Ordnung.** [aləs ist ɪn ˈɔʁdnʊŋ]

Come here, please.

Kommen Sie bitte her.
[kɔmən zi: 'bɪtə he:ɐ]

I have some questions for you.

Ich habe einige Fragen für Sie.
[ɪç 'ha:bə 'aɪnɪgə 'fʀa:gən fy:ɐ zi:]

Wait a moment, please.

Warten Sie einen Moment bitte.
[vaʁtən 'aɪnən mɔ'mɛnt 'bɪtə]

Do you have any I.D.?

Haben Sie einen Ausweis?
[ha:bən zi: 'aɪnən 'aʊsˌvaɪs?]

Thanks. You can leave now.

Danke. Sie können nun gehen.
[daŋkə. zi: 'kœnən nu:n 'ge:ən]

Hands behind your head!

Hände hinter dem Kopf!
[hɛndə 'hɪntɐ dem kɔpf!]

You're under arrest!

Sie sind verhaftet!
[zi: zɪnt fɛɐ'haftət!]

Health problems

Please help me.	**Helfen Sie mir bitte.** [hɛlfən zi: mi:ɐ 'bɪtə]
I don't feel well.	**Mir ist schlecht.** [mi:ɐ ɪs ʃlɛçt]
My husband doesn't feel well.	**Meinem Ehemann ist schlecht.** [maɪnəm 'e:əman ist ʃlɛçt]
My son ...	**Mein Sohn ...** [maɪn zo:n ...]
My father ...	**Mein Vater ...** [maɪn 'fa:tɐ ...]
My wife doesn't feel well.	**Meine Frau fühlt sich nicht gut.** [maɪnə 'fʀaʊ fy:lt zɪç nɪçt gu:t]
My daughter ...	**Meine Tochter ...** [maɪnə 'tɔχtɐ ...]
My mother ...	**Meine Mutter ...** [maɪnə 'mʊtɐ ...]
I've got a ...	**Ich habe ... schmerzen.** [ɪç 'ha:bə ... 'ʃmɛʁtsən]
headache	**Kopf-** [kɔpf]
sore throat	**Hals-** [hals]
stomach ache	**Bauch-** [baʊχ]
toothache	**Zahn-** [tsa:n]
I feel dizzy.	**Mir ist schwindelig.** [mi:ɐ ɪs 'ʃvɪndəlɪç]
He has a fever.	**Er hat Fieber.** [e:ɐ hat 'fi:bɐ]
She has a fever.	**Sie hat Fieber.** [zi: hat 'fi:bɐ]
I can't breathe.	**Ich kann nicht atmen.** [ɪç kan nɪçt 'a:tmən]
I'm short of breath.	**Ich kriege keine Luft.** [ɪç 'kʀi:gə 'kaɪnə lʊft]
I am asthmatic.	**Ich bin Asthmatiker.** [ɪç bɪn ast'ma:tikɐ]
I am diabetic.	**Ich bin Diabetiker /Diabetikerin/** [ɪç bɪn dia'be:tikɐ /dia'be:tikəʀɪn/]

I can't sleep.

Ich habe Schlaflosigkeit.
[ɪç 'ha:bə 'ʃla:flo:zɪçkaɪt]

food poisoning

Lebensmittelvergiftung
[le:bəns‚mɪtəl·fɛɐ‚gɪftʊŋ]

It hurts here.

Es tut hier weh.
[ɛs tʊt hi:ɐ ve:]

Help me!

Hilfe!
[hɪlfə!]

I am here!

Ich bin hier!
[ɪç bɪn hi:ɐ!]

We are here!

Wir sind hier!
[vi:ɐ zɪnt hi:ɐ!]

Get me out of here!

Bringen Sie mich hier raus!
[bʀɪŋən zi: mɪç hi:ɐ 'ʀaʊs!]

I need a doctor.

Ich brauche einen Arzt.
[ɪç 'bʀaʊxə 'aɪnən aʁtst]

I can't move.

Ich kann mich nicht bewegen.
[ɪç kan mɪç nɪçt bə've:gən]

I can't move my legs.

Ich kann meine Beine nicht bewegen.
[ɪç kan 'maɪnə 'baɪnə nɪçt bə've:gən]

I have a wound.

Ich habe eine Wunde.
[ɪç 'ha:bə 'aɪnə 'vʊndə]

Is it serious?

Ist es ernst?
[ist ɛs ɛʁnst?]

My documents are in my pocket.

Meine Dokumente sind in meiner Hosentasche.
[maɪnə doku'mɛntə zɪnt ɪn 'maɪnə 'ho:zən‚taʃə]

Calm down!

Beruhigen Sie sich!
[bə'ʀu:ɪgən zi: zɪç!]

May I use your phone?

Kann ich Ihr Telefon benutzen?
[kan ɪç i:ɐ tele'fo:n bə'nʊtsən?]

Call an ambulance!

Rufen Sie einen Krankenwagen!
[ʀu:fən zi: 'aɪnən 'kʀaŋkən‚va:gən!]

It's urgent!

Es ist dringend!
[ɛs ist 'dʀɪŋənt!]

It's an emergency!

Es ist ein Notfall!
[ɛs ist aɪn 'no:t‚fal!]

Please hurry up!

Schneller bitte!
[ʃnɛlɐ 'bɪtə!]

Would you please call a doctor?

Können Sie bitte einen Arzt rufen?
[kœnən zi: 'bɪtə 'aɪnən aʁtst 'ʀu:fən?]

Where is the hospital?

Wo ist das Krankenhaus?
[vo: ist das 'kʀaŋkən‚haʊs?]

How are you feeling?

Wie fühlen Sie sich?
[vi: 'fy:lən zi: zɪç?]

Are you all right?

Ist bei Ihnen alles in Ordnung?
[ist baɪ 'i:nən 'aləs ɪn 'ɔʁdnʊŋ?]

What's happened?	**Was ist passiert?** [vas ɪst pa'siːɐt?]
I feel better now.	**Mir geht es schon besser.** [miːɐ geːt ɛs ʃoːn 'bɛsɐ]
It's OK.	**Es ist in Ordnung.** [ɛs ist ɪn 'ɔʁdnʊŋ]
It's all right.	**Alles ist in Ordnung.** [aləs ist ɪn 'ɔʁdnʊŋ]

At the pharmacy

pharmacy (drugstore)	**Apotheke** [apo'te:kə]
24-hour pharmacy	**24 Stunden Apotheke** [fi:ɐ·ʊn·'tsvantsɪç 'ʃtʊndən apo'te:kə]
Where is the closest pharmacy?	**Wo ist die nächste Apotheke?** [vo: ist di 'nɛ:çstə apo'te:kə?]
Is it open now?	**Ist sie jetzt offen?** [ist zi: jɛtst 'ɔfən?]
At what time does it open?	**Um wie viel Uhr öffnet sie?** [ʊm vifi:l u:ɐ 'œfnət zi:?]
At what time does it close?	**Um wie viel Uhr schließt sie?** [ʊm vifi:l u:ɐ ʃli:st zi:?]
Is it far?	**Ist es weit?** [ist ɛs vaɪt?]
Can I get there on foot?	**Kann ich dort zu Fuß hingehen?** [kan ɪç dɔɐt tsu fu:s 'hɪnˌge:ən?]
Can you show me on the map?	**Können Sie es mir auf der Karte zeigen?** [kœnən zi: ɛs mi:ɐ aʊf de:ɐ 'kaʁtə 'tsaɪgən?]
Please give me something for ...	**Bitte geben sie mir etwas gegen ...** [bɪtə ge:bn zi: mi:ɐ 'ɛtvas 'ge:gən ...]
a headache	**Kopfschmerzen** [kɔpfˌʃmɛʁtsən]
a cough	**Husten** [hu:stən]
a cold	**eine Erkältung** [aɪnə ɛɐ'kɛltʊn]
the flu	**die Grippe** [di 'gʁɪpə]
a fever	**Fieber** [fi:bɐ]
a stomach ache	**Magenschmerzen** [ma:gənˌʃmɛʁtsən]
nausea	**Übelkeit** [y:bəlkaɪt]
diarrhea	**Durchfall** [dʊʁçˌfal]
constipation	**Verstopfung** [fɛɐ'ʃtɔpfʊn]

pain in the back	**Rückenschmerzen** [ʀʏkən‿ʃmɛʀtsən]
chest pain	**Brustschmerzen** [bʀʊstʃmɛʀtsən]
side stitch	**Seitenstechen** [zaɪtənʃteçən]
abdominal pain	**Bauchschmerzen** [baʊχʃmɛʀtsən]

pill	**Pille** [pɪlə]
ointment, cream	**Salbe, Creme** [zalbə, kʀɛːm]
syrup	**Sirup** [ziːʀʊp]
spray	**Spray** [ʃpʀeː]
drops	**Tropfen** [tʀɔpfən]

You need to go to the hospital.	**Sie müssen ins Krankenhaus gehen.** [ziː 'mʏsən ɪns 'kʀaŋkən‿haʊs 'geːən]
health insurance	**Krankenversicherung** [kʀaŋkən·fɛɐ̯ˌzɪçəʀʊŋ]
prescription	**Rezept** [ʀeˈtsɛpt]
insect repellant	**Insektenschutzmittel** [ɪnˈzɛktən·ˈʃʊtsˌmɪtəl]
Band Aid	**Pflaster** [pflastə]

The bare minimum

Excuse me, ...
Entschuldigen Sie bitte, ...
[ɛnt'ʃʊldɪgən zi: 'bɪtə, ...]

Hello.
Hallo.
[ha'lo:]

Thank you.
Danke.
[daŋkə]

Good bye.
Auf Wiedersehen.
[aʊf 'vi:dɐˌze:ən]

Yes.
Ja.
[ja:]

No.
Nein.
[naɪn]

I don't know.
Ich weiß nicht.
[ɪç vaɪs nɪçt]

Where? | Where to? | When?
Wo? | Wohin? | Wann?
[vo:? | vo'hɪn? | van?]

I need ...
Ich brauche ...
[ɪç 'bʀaʊxə ...]

I want ...
Ich möchte ...
[ɪç 'mœçtə ...]

Do you have ...?
Haben Sie ...?
[ha:bən zi: ...?]

Is there a ... here?
Gibt es hier ...?
[gi:pt ɛs hi:ɐ ...?]

May I ...?
Kann ich ...?
[kan ɪç ...?]

..., please (polite request)
Bitte
[bɪtə]

I'm looking for ...
Ich suche ...
[ɪç 'zu:xə ...]

the restroom
Toilette
[toa'lɛtə]

an ATM
Geldautomat
[gɛlt?aʊtoˌma:t]

a pharmacy (drugstore)
Apotheke
[apo'te:kə]

a hospital
Krankenhaus
[kʀaŋkənˌhaʊs]

the police station
Polizeistation
[poli'tsaɪˌʃtaˌtsjo:n]

the subway
U-Bahn
[u:ba:n]

a taxi	**Taxi** [taksi]
the train station	**Bahnhof** [ba:n,ho:f]

My name is ...	**Ich heiße ...** [ɪç 'haɪsə ...]
What's your name?	**Wie heißen Sie?** [vi: 'haɪsən zi:?]
Could you please help me?	**Helfen Sie mir bitte.** [hɛlfən zi: mi:ɐ 'bɪtə]
I've got a problem.	**Ich habe ein Problem.** [ɪç 'ha:bə aɪn pʀo'ble:m]
I don't feel well.	**Mir ist schlecht.** [mi:ɐ ɪs ʃlɛçt]
Call an ambulance!	**Rufen Sie einen Krankenwagen!** [ʀu:fən zi: 'aɪnən 'kʀaŋkən,va:gən!]
May I make a call?	**Darf ich telefonieren?** [daʀf ɪç telefo'ni:ʀən?]

I'm sorry.	**Entschuldigung.** [ɛnt'ʃuldɪgʊŋ]
You're welcome.	**Keine Ursache.** [kaɪnə 'u:ɐ,zaχə]

I, me	**ich** [ɪç]
you (inform.)	**du** [du:]
he	**er** [e:ɐ]
she	**sie** [zi:]
they (masc.)	**sie** [zi:]
they (fem.)	**sie** [zi:]
we	**wir** [vi:ɐ]
you (pl)	**ihr** [i:ɐ]
you (sg, form.)	**Sie** [zi:]

ENTRANCE	**EINGANG** [aɪn,gaŋ]
EXIT	**AUSGANG** [aʊs,gaŋ]
OUT OF ORDER	**AUßER BETRIEB** [,aʊsɐ bə'tʀi:p]
CLOSED	**GESCHLOSSEN** [gə'ʃlɔsən]

OPEN	**OFFEN** [ɔfən]
FOR WOMEN	**FÜR DAMEN** [fyːɐ 'damən]
FOR MEN	**FÜR HERREN** [fyːɐ 'hɛʀən]

MINI DICTIONARY

This section contains 250 useful words required for everyday communication. You will find the names of months and days of the week here. The dictionary also contains topics such as colors, measurements, family, and more

T&P Books Publishing

DICTIONARY CONTENTS

T&P Books Publishing

time	**Zeit** (f)	[tsaɪt]
hour	**Stunde** (f)	[ˈʃtʊndə]
half an hour	**eine halbe Stunde**	[ˈaɪnə ˈhalbə ˈʃtʊndə]
minute	**Minute** (f)	[miˈnuːtə]
second	**Sekunde** (f)	[zeˈkʊndə]

today (adv)	**heute**	[ˈhɔɪtə]
tomorrow (adv)	**morgen**	[ˈmɔʁɡən]
yesterday (adv)	**gestern**	[ˈɡɛstɐn]

Monday	**Montag** (m)	[ˈmoːntaːk]
Tuesday	**Dienstag** (m)	[ˈdiːnstaːk]
Wednesday	**Mittwoch** (m)	[ˈmɪtvɔχ]
Thursday	**Donnerstag** (m)	[ˈdɔnɐstaːk]
Friday	**Freitag** (m)	[ˈfʁaɪtaːk]
Saturday	**Samstag** (m)	[ˈzamstaːk]
Sunday	**Sonntag** (m)	[ˈzɔntaːk]

day	**Tag** (m)	[taːk]
working day	**Arbeitstag** (m)	[ˈaʁbaɪtsˌtaːk]
public holiday	**Feiertag** (m)	[ˈfaɪɐˌtaːk]
weekend	**Wochenende** (n)	[ˈvɔχənˌʔɛndə]

week	**Woche** (f)	[ˈvɔχə]
last week (adv)	**letzte Woche**	[ˈlɛtstə ˈvɔχə]
next week (adv)	**nächste Woche**	[ˈnɛːçstə ˈvɔχə]

| in the morning | **morgens** | [ˈmɔʁɡəns] |
| in the afternoon | **nachmittags** | [ˈnaχmɪˌtaːks] |

| in the evening | **abends** | [ˈaːbənts] |
| tonight (this evening) | **heute Abend** | [ˈhɔɪtə ˈaːbənt] |

| at night | **nachts** | [naχts] |
| midnight | **Mitternacht** (f) | [ˈmɪtɐˌnaχt] |

January	**Januar** (m)	[ˈjanuaːɐ]
February	**Februar** (m)	[ˈfeːbʁuaːɐ]
March	**März** (m)	[mɛʁts]
April	**April** (m)	[aˈpʁɪl]
May	**Mai** (m)	[maɪ]
June	**Juni** (m)	[ˈjuːni]

| July | **Juli** (m) | [ˈjuːli] |
| August | **August** (m) | [aʊˈɡʊst] |

September	September (m)	[zɛp'tɛmbɐ]
October	Oktober (m)	[ɔk'to:bɐ]
November	November (m)	[no'vɛmbɐ]
December	Dezember (m)	[de'tsɛmbɐ]

in spring	im Frühling	[ɪm 'fʀy:lɪŋ]
in summer	im Sommer	[ɪm 'zɔmɐ]
in fall	im Herbst	[ɪm hɛʁpst]
in winter	im Winter	[ɪm 'vɪntɐ]

month	Monat (m)	['mo:nat]
season (summer, etc.)	Saison (f)	[zɛ'zɔŋ]
year	Jahr (n)	[ja:ɐ]

2. Numbers. Numerals

0 zero	null	[nʊl]
1 one	eins	[aɪns]
2 two	zwei	[tsvaɪ]
3 three	drei	[dʀaɪ]
4 four	vier	[fi:ɐ]

5 five	fünf	[fʏnf]
6 six	sechs	[zɛks]
7 seven	sieben	['zi:bən]
8 eight	acht	[aχt]
9 nine	neun	[nɔɪn]
10 ten	zehn	[tse:n]

11 eleven	elf	[ɛlf]
12 twelve	zwölf	[tsvœlf]
13 thirteen	dreizehn	['dʀaɪtse:n]
14 fourteen	vierzehn	['fiʁtse:n]
15 fifteen	fünfzehn	['fʏnftse:n]

16 sixteen	sechzehn	['zɛçtse:n]
17 seventeen	siebzehn	['zi:ptse:n]
18 eighteen	achtzehn	['aχtse:n]
19 nineteen	neunzehn	['nɔɪntse:n]

20 twenty	zwanzig	['tsvantsɪç]
30 thirty	dreißig	['dʀaɪsɪç]
40 forty	vierzig	['fiʁtsɪç]
50 fifty	fünfzig	['fʏnftsɪç]

60 sixty	sechzig	['zɛçtsɪç]
70 seventy	siebzig	['zi:ptsɪç]
80 eighty	achtzig	['aχtsɪç]
90 ninety	neunzig	['nɔɪntsɪç]
100 one hundred	einhundert	['aɪn,hʊndɐt]

200 two hundred	**zweihundert**	['tsvaɪˌhʊndət]
300 three hundred	**dreihundert**	['dʀaɪˌhʊndət]
400 four hundred	**vierhundert**	['fiːɐˌhʊndət]
500 five hundred	**fünfhundert**	['fʏnfˌhʊndət]
600 six hundred	**sechshundert**	[zɛksˌhʊndət]
700 seven hundred	**siebenhundert**	['ziːbənˌhʊndət]
800 eight hundred	**achthundert**	['axtˌhʊndət]
900 nine hundred	**neunhundert**	['nɔɪnˌhʊndət]
1000 one thousand	**eintausend**	['aɪnˌtaʊzənt]
10000 ten thousand	**zehntausend**	['tsenˌtaʊzənt]
one hundred thousand	**hunderttausend**	['hʊndətˌtaʊzənt]
million	**Million** (f)	[mɪ'ljoːn]
billion	**Milliarde** (f)	[mɪ'lɪaʀdə]

3. Humans. Family

man (adult male)	**Mann** (m)	[man]
young man	**Junge** (m)	['jʊŋə]
woman	**Frau** (f)	[fʀaʊ]
girl (young woman)	**Mädchen** (n)	['mɛːtçən]
old man	**Greis** (m)	[gʀaɪs]
old woman	**alte Frau** (f)	['altə 'fʀaʊ]
mother	**Mutter** (f)	['mʊtə]
father	**Vater** (m)	['faːtə]
son	**Sohn** (m)	[zoːn]
daughter	**Tochter** (f)	['tɔxtə]
brother	**Bruder** (m)	['bʀuːdə]
sister	**Schwester** (f)	['ʃvɛstə]
parents	**Eltern** (pl)	['ɛltən]
child	**Kind** (n)	[kɪnt]
children	**Kinder** (pl)	['kɪndə]
stepmother	**Stiefmutter** (f)	['ʃtiːfˌmʊtə]
stepfather	**Stiefvater** (m)	['ʃtiːfˌfaːtə]
grandmother	**Großmutter** (f)	['gʀoːsˌmʊtə]
grandfather	**Großvater** (m)	['gʀoːsˌfaːtə]
grandson	**Enkel** (m)	['ɛŋkəl]
granddaughter	**Enkelin** (f)	['ɛŋkəlɪn]
grandchildren	**Enkelkinder** (pl)	['ɛŋkəlˌkɪndə]
uncle	**Onkel** (m)	['ɔŋkəl]
aunt	**Tante** (f)	['tantə]
nephew	**Neffe** (m)	['nɛfə]
niece	**Nichte** (f)	['nɪçtə]
wife	**Frau** (f)	[fʀaʊ]

husband	**Mann** (m)	[man]
married (masc.)	**verheiratet**	[fɛɛ'haɪʀaːtət]
married (fem.)	**verheiratet**	[fɛɛ'haɪʀaːtət]
widow	**Witwe** (f)	['vɪtvə]
widower	**Witwer** (m)	['vɪtvɐ]

| name (first name) | **Vorname** (m) | ['foːɐˌnaːmə] |
| surname (last name) | **Name** (m) | ['naːmə] |

relative	**Verwandte** (m)	[fɛɛ'vantə]
friend (masc.)	**Freund** (m)	[fʀɔɪnt]
friendship	**Freundschaft** (f)	['fʀɔɪntʃaft]

partner	**Partner** (m)	['paʁtnɐ]
superior (n)	**Vorgesetzte** (m)	['foːɐɡəˌzɛtstə]
colleague	**Kollege** (m), **Kollegin** (f)	[kɔ'leːɡə], [kɔ'leːɡɪn]
neighbors	**Nachbarn** (pl)	['naχbaːɐn]

4. Human body

body	**Körper** (m)	['kœʁpɐ]
heart	**Herz** (n)	[hɛʁts]
blood	**Blut** (n)	[bluːt]
brain	**Gehirn** (n)	[ɡə'hɪʁn]

bone	**Knochen** (m)	['knɔχən]
spine (backbone)	**Wirbelsäule** (f)	['vɪʁbəlˌzɔɪlə]
rib	**Rippe** (f)	['ʀɪpə]
lungs	**Lungen** (pl)	['lʊŋən]
skin	**Haut** (f)	[haʊt]

head	**Kopf** (m)	[kɔpf]
face	**Gesicht** (n)	[ɡə'zɪçt]
nose	**Nase** (f)	['naːzə]
forehead	**Stirn** (f)	[ʃtɪʁn]
cheek	**Wange** (f)	['vaŋə]

mouth	**Mund** (m)	[mʊnt]
tongue	**Zunge** (f)	['tsʊŋə]
tooth	**Zahn** (m)	[tsaːn]
lips	**Lippen** (pl)	['lɪpən]
chin	**Kinn** (n)	[kɪn]

ear	**Ohr** (n)	[oːɐ]
neck	**Hals** (m)	[hals]
eye	**Auge** (n)	['aʊɡə]
pupil	**Pupille** (f)	[pu'pɪlə]
eyebrow	**Augenbraue** (f)	['aʊɡənˌbʀaʊə]
eyelash	**Wimper** (f)	['vɪmpɐ]
hair	**Haare** (pl)	['haːʀə]

hairstyle	**Frisur** (f)	[ˌfʀiˈzuːɐ]
mustache	**Schnurrbart** (m)	[ˈʃnʊʀˌbaːɐt]
beard	**Bart** (m)	[baːɐt]
to have (a beard, etc.)	**haben** (vt)	[haːbən]
bald (adj)	**kahl**	[kaːl]

hand	**Hand** (f)	[hant]
arm	**Arm** (m)	[aʀm]
finger	**Finger** (m)	[ˈfɪŋɐ]
nail	**Nagel** (m)	[ˈnaːɡəl]
palm	**Handfläche** (f)	[ˈhant·ˌflɛçə]

shoulder	**Schulter** (f)	[ˈʃʊltɐ]
leg	**Bein** (n)	[baɪn]
knee	**Knie** (n)	[kniː]
heel	**Ferse** (f)	[ˈfɛʀzə]
back	**Rücken** (m)	[ˈʀʏkən]

5. Clothing. Personal accessories

clothes	**Kleidung** (f)	[ˈklaɪdʊŋ]
coat (overcoat)	**Mantel** (m)	[ˈmantəl]
fur coat	**Pelzmantel** (m)	[ˈpɛltsˌmantəl]
jacket (e.g., leather ~)	**Jacke** (f)	[ˈjakə]
raincoat (trenchcoat, etc.)	**Regenmantel** (m)	[ˈʀeːɡənˌmantəl]

shirt (button shirt)	**Hemd** (n)	[hɛmt]
pants	**Hose** (f)	[ˈhoːzə]
suit jacket	**Jackett** (n)	[ʒaˈkɛt]
suit	**Anzug** (m)	[ˈanˌtsuːk]

dress (frock)	**Kleid** (n)	[klaɪt]
skirt	**Rock** (m)	[ʀɔk]
T-shirt	**T-Shirt** (n)	[ˈtiːˌʃøːɐt]
bathrobe	**Bademantel** (m)	[ˈbaːdəˌmantəl]
pajamas	**Schlafanzug** (m)	[ˈʃlaːfʔanˌtsuːk]
workwear	**Arbeitskleidung** (f)	[ˈaʀbaɪtsˌklaɪdʊŋ]

underwear	**Unterwäsche** (f)	[ˈʊntɐˌvɛʃə]
socks	**Socken** (pl)	[ˈzɔkən]
bra	**Büstenhalter** (m)	[ˈbystənˌhaltɐ]
pantyhose	**Strumpfhose** (f)	[ˈʃtʀʊmpfˌhoːzə]
stockings (thigh highs)	**Strümpfe** (pl)	[ˈʃtʀʏmpfə]
bathing suit	**Badeanzug** (m)	[ˈbaːdəˌʔantsuːk]

hat	**Mütze** (f)	[ˈmʏtsə]
footwear	**Schuhe** (pl)	[ˈʃuːə]
boots (e.g., cowboy ~)	**Stiefel** (pl)	[ˈʃtiːfəl]
heel	**Absatz** (m)	[ˈapˌzats]
shoestring	**Schnürsenkel** (m)	[ˈʃnyːɐˌsɛŋkəl]

shoe polish	**Schuhcreme** (f)	['ʃu:ˌkʀɛ:m]
gloves	**Handschuhe** (pl)	['hantˌʃu:ə]
mittens	**Fausthandschuhe** (pl)	['faʊst·hantˌʃu:ə]
scarf (muffler)	**Schal** (m)	[ʃa:l]
glasses (eyeglasses)	**Brille** (f)	['bʀɪlə]
umbrella	**Regenschirm** (m)	['ʀe:gənˌʃɪʀm]
tie (necktie)	**Krawatte** (f)	[kʀa'vatə]
handkerchief	**Taschentuch** (n)	['taʃənˌtu:x]
comb	**Kamm** (m)	[kam]
hairbrush	**Haarbürste** (f)	['ha:ɐˌbʏʀstə]
buckle	**Schnalle** (f)	['ʃnalə]
belt	**Gürtel** (m)	['gʏʀtəl]
purse	**Handtasche** (f)	['hantˌtaʃə]

6. House. Apartment

apartment	**Wohnung** (f)	['vo:nʊŋ]
room	**Zimmer** (n)	['tsɪmɐ]
bedroom	**Schlafzimmer** (n)	['ʃla:fˌtsɪmɐ]
dining room	**Esszimmer** (n)	['ɛsˌtsɪmɐ]
living room	**Wohnzimmer** (n)	['vo:nˌtsɪmɐ]
study (home office)	**Arbeitszimmer** (n)	['aʀbaɪtsˌtsɪmɐ]
entry room	**Vorzimmer** (n)	['fo:ɐˌtsɪmɐ]
bathroom (room with a bath or shower)	**Badezimmer** (n)	['ba:dəˌtsɪmɐ]
half bath	**Toilette** (f)	[toa'lɛtə]
vacuum cleaner	**Staubsauger** (m)	['ʃtaʊpˌzaʊgɐ]
mop	**Schrubber** (m)	['ʃʀʊbɐ]
dust cloth	**Lappen** (m)	['lapən]
short broom	**Besen** (m)	['be:zən]
dustpan	**Kehrichtschaufel** (f)	['ke:ʀɪçtˌʃaʊfəl]
furniture	**Möbel** (n)	['mø:bəl]
table	**Tisch** (m)	[tɪʃ]
chair	**Stuhl** (m)	[ʃtu:l]
armchair	**Sessel** (m)	['zɛsəl]
mirror	**Spiegel** (m)	['ʃpi:gəl]
carpet	**Teppich** (m)	['tɛpɪç]
fireplace	**Kamin** (m)	[ka'mi:n]
drapes	**Vorhänge** (pl)	['fo:ɐhɛŋə]
table lamp	**Tischlampe** (f)	['tɪʃˌlampə]
chandelier	**Kronleuchter** (m)	['kʀo:nˌlɔɪçtɐ]
kitchen	**Küche** (f)	['kʏçə]
gas stove (range)	**Gasherd** (m)	['ga:sˌhe:ɐt]

| electric stove | Elektroherd (m) | [e'lɛktʀoˌheːɐt] |
| microwave oven | Mikrowellenherd (m) | ['mikʀovɛlənˌheːɐt] |

refrigerator	Kühlschrank (m)	['kyːlʃʀaŋk]
freezer	Tiefkühltruhe (f)	['tiːfkyːlˌtʀuːə]
dishwasher	Geschirrspülmaschine (f)	[gə'ʃɪʁˈʃpyːl·maˌʃiːnə]
faucet	Wasserhahn (m)	['vasɐˌhaːn]

meat grinder	Fleischwolf (m)	['flaɪʃvolf]
juicer	Saftpresse (f)	['zaftˌpʀɛsə]
toaster	Toaster (m)	['toːstɐ]
mixer	Mixer (m)	['mɪksɐ]

coffee machine	Kaffeemaschine (f)	['kafe·maˌʃiːnə]
kettle	Wasserkessel (m)	['vasɐˌkɛsəl]
teapot	Teekanne (f)	['teːˌkanə]

TV set	Fernseher (m)	['fɛʁnˌzeːɐ]
VCR (video recorder)	Videorekorder (m)	['video·ʀeˌkɔʁdɐ]
iron (e.g., steam ~)	Bügeleisen (n)	['byːgəlˌʔaɪzən]
telephone	Telefon (n)	[tele'foːn]